AUTHENTIC TEXAS
CAFES

AUTHENTIC TEXAS
CAFES

SUSAN ELLIS KENNARD
AND ED KENNARD

★
TexasMonthlyPress

Map illustrations by B&H Design+Drafting

Copyright © 1986 by Susan Ellis Kennard and Ed Kennard. All rights including reproduction by photographic or electronic process and translation into other languages are fully reserved under the International Copyright Union, the Universal Copyright Convention, and the Pan-American Copyright Convention. Reproduction or use of this book in whole or in part in any manner without written permission of the publisher is strictly prohibited.

Texas Monthly Press, Inc.
P.O. Box 1569
Austin, Texas 78767

A B C D E F G H

Library of Congress Cataloging-in-Publication Data

Kennard, Susan Ellis, 1947-
   Authentic Texas cafes.

   Expansion of an article that originally appeared
in the July 1984 issue of Texas Monthly.
   1. Restaurants, lunch rooms, etc.—Texas—Directories.
I. Kennard, Ed, 1945-   . II. Title.
TX907.K425 1986   647'.95764   86-5984
ISBN 0-87719-053-4

To Ashley and Drew

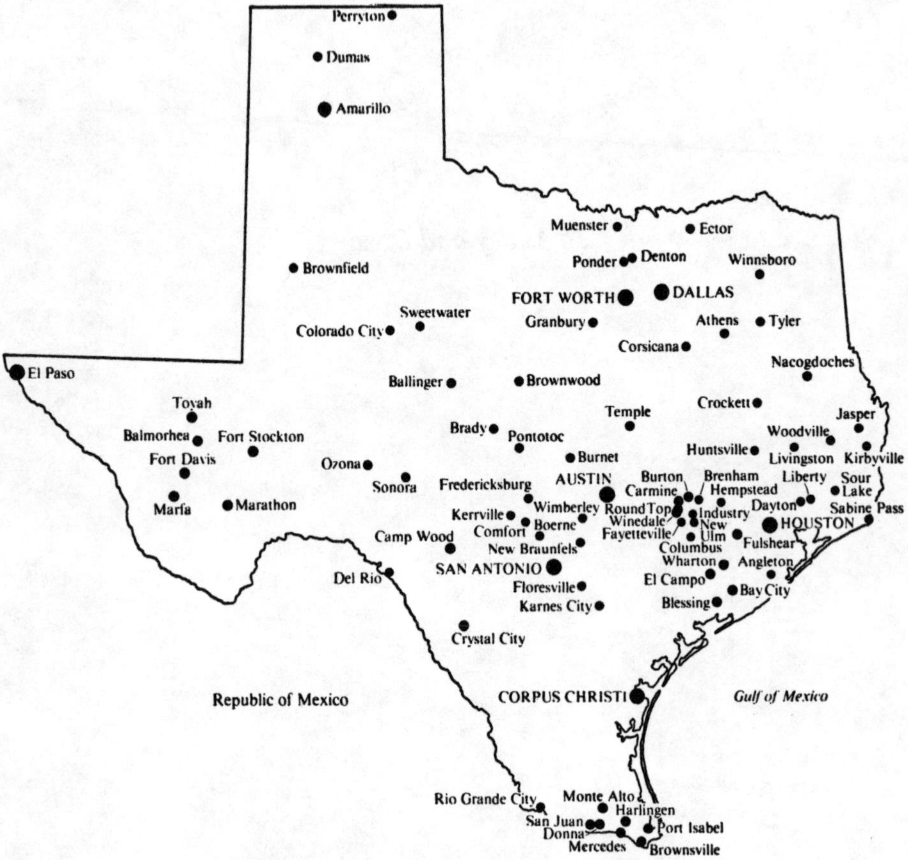
Perryton
Dumas
Amarillo
Muenster
Ector
Ponder
Denton
Winnsboro
Brownfield
FORT WORTH
DALLAS
Sweetwater
Colorado City
Granbury
Athens
Tyler
Corsicana
El Paso
Nacogdoches
Ballinger
Brownwood
Toyah
Temple
Crockett
Jasper
Balmorhea
Fort Stockton
Brady
Pontotoc
Woodville
Huntsville
Fort Davis
Burnet
Livingston
Kirbyville
Ozona
AUSTIN
Burton
Brenham
Liberty
Sour Lake
Sonora
Fredericksburg
Carmine
Hempstead
Marfa
Marathon
Wimberley
Round Top
Industry
Dayton
Sabine Pass
Kerrville
Boerne
Winedale
New Ulm
HOUSTON
Camp Wood
Comfort
Fayetteville
Columbus
Fulshear
New Braunfels
Wharton
Angleton
SAN ANTONIO
Del Rio
El Campo
Floresville
Bay City
Karnes City
Blessing
Crystal City
Republic of Mexico
CORPUS CHRISTI
Gulf of Mexico
Rio Grande City
Monte Alto
Harlingen
San Juan
Port Isabel
Donna
Mercedes
Brownsville

CONTENTS

Acknowledgments xi
Introduction 1
PANHANDLE 7
    Map 8
    Amarillo 9
    Brownfield 13
    Dumas 15
    Perryton 17
NORTH/NORTHEAST 19
    Map 20
    Athens 21
    Corsicana 23
    Denton 25
    Ector 29
    Granbury 31
    Muenster 35
    Nacogdoches 37
    Ponder 39
    Tyler 41
    Winnsboro 43
CENTRAL 45
    Map 46
    Boerne 47
    Brady 49
    Brownwood 51
    Burnet 53
    Comfort 55
    Floresville 57
    Fredericksburg 59
    Karnes City 61
    Kerrville 63
    New Braunfels 65
    Pontotoc 67
    Temple 69
    Wimberley 71
SOUTHEAST 73
    Map 74
    Angleton 75
    Bay City 77
    Blessing 79

Brenham	81
Burton	83
Carmine	85
Columbus	87
Crockett	89
Dayton	91
El Campo	93
Fayetteville	95
Fulshear	97
Hempstead	99
Huntsville	101
Industry	103
Jasper	105
Kirbyville	107
Liberty	109
Livingston	111
New Ulm	113
Round Top	115
Sabine Pass	117
Sour Lake	121
Wharton	123
Winedale	125
Woodville	127
SOUTH	131
Map	132
Brownsville	133
Crystal City	135
Donna	137
Harlingen	139
Mercedes	141
Monte Alto	143
Port Isabel	145
Rio Grande City	147
San Juan	149
WEST	151
Map	152
Ballinger	153
Balmorhea	155
Camp Wood	157
Colorado City	159
Del Rio	161
El Paso	163
Fort Davis	165
Fort Stockton	167

  Marathon 171
  Marfa 173
  Ozona 175
  Sonora 177
  Sweetwater 179
  Toyah 181
CITIES 183
  Austin 185
  Corpus Christi 189
  Dallas 191
  Fort Worth 195
  Houston 197
  San Antonio 201

Acknowledgments

Many thanks to the following people who gave us sage advice and continuing support, intertwined with good judgment: Peter Applebome, Marion Barthelme, Marge and Calvin Bentsen, Greg Curtis, Nick and Mary Kate Feild, Vreni Guggenbuhl, Peggy and Ed Hennessy, Mike Hicks, Nathalie and Mont Hoyt, Jonas Kennard, Richard and Brenda Kilmer, Peggy and Billy Oehmig, Joan and Jack Onder, Suzi Sands, Janice Schindler, and Pat Sharpe.

Introduction

This book began innocently enough. As my wife Susan and I were driving with our daughter Ashley through the Panhandle on our way to a Colorado summer vacation, I remarked that we should write an article for *Texas Monthly* magazine listing cafes and restaurants in small towns throughout the state that we felt served good food. This, I went on to explain, would give motorists such as ourselves an alternative to fast-food restaurants along the highways.

Susan warmed to the idea, as did Greg Curtis, editor-in-chief of the magazine. Our Texas cafe article appeared in the July 1984 issue as the cover story. Because of the success of that article, we subsequently decided to expand it into a book.

The trouble with writing an article such as that or a book such as this is quite obvious. It takes an incredible amount of time and effort to drive around this great big state of ours and eat at hundreds of cafes and interview their owners. But that's exactly what Susan did. She drove thousands of miles through all parts of the state, following one lead after another.

My own qualification for writing this book is simply that I have always been a cafe lover. It has something to do with my childhood. Every morning during my summer visits to Anderson, Texas, my grandfather would take me to a cafe where I would watch him drink coffee as he talked to other men. I have also tried to read every book on the subject of country food and cafes I could find. I got involved in this book because I think Texans deserve a food book such as this.

I can tell you for a fact that Susan gained (and later lost) more than fifteen pounds as a result of her research. In every case her routine was the same. She would first eat the food, and if the food was good, she would interview the owners if that was practical. Sometimes the proprietors were too busy or Susan just had to get on down the road. When this happened, she telephoned them later.

I can remember countless late-night phone calls during which Susan would describe how she had found a cafe here that had drilled holes in the floor because of a flood in 1900, or a cafe there that was so filthy she wouldn't even touch her knife and fork. (The latter kind are not listed here!) She met some fascinating people along the way, many of whom I am sure she will not soon forget.

So how did a cafe or country restaurant make it into this guidebook? Beyond the obvious points that every cafe had to be clean and a place you could bring your family, they had to qualify in one of three categories: food, atmosphere, or something very unusual. Food is obviously the first reason anybody would want to buy and use this book. It was therefore our ambition from the beginning not to compromise in this area. We looked for cafes that strived as much as possible to cook food that used fresh ingredients, that tried to avoid canned vegetables and frozen precut and ready-to-cook french fries, meats, and seafood. What we discovered is that there are hundreds of people out there doing their best to serve good food. Some of these folks had to cut a corner here or there, but as long as it wasn't major, we deemed it okay. Indeed, if all cafe owners had to make every item from absolute scratch, they probably wouldn't be around for long. But by and large, these people are still cooking food as we think it should be cooked. And it's these people we have included.

We've heard debates about the subject of atmosphere, but we think atmosphere has a lot to do with the taste of food. So naturally Susan and I felt that atmosphere was also important in considering whether a cafe was one we would recommend. A restaurant that has both good food and good atmosphere is generally a great deal more successful than restaurants that just have good food or good atmosphere. There's a powerful synergy here. To see a few examples, drop into the Fisherman's Inn in Port

Isabel, Chicken Charlie's in Balmorhea, or Caro's in Rio Grande City. I could name many more, but you get the point. Atmosphere as well as good food is what most cafes in this book are all about.

In a couple of cases, we included a restaurant here or there that we felt was worthy of mention for some other reason. When that happened, we have noted the reason and advised the reader accordingly.

After assembling our final list of cafes, we were somewhat disappointed to find that it did not approach the numbers included in other books on this subject. Our disappointment faded quickly, however, when we reminded ourselves that all along we had been trying not for quantity, but rather for quality. It is our view that the readers of this book will be looking for that something extra when they walk into a cafe, and that's what we feel anyone who uses this book will experience. We have edited the state of Texas for you so you don't have to stumble into a room full of hostile people eating food you wouldn't serve to your pet beagle. We think every cafe in this book is a special place.

On a practical note, we have made no attempt to list whether the cafe or restaurant takes credit cards because in most cases they don't. Eating a three-dollar breakfast in a cafe is a cash event. It makes little sense, when you think about it, for a cafe owner to offer Visa or MasterCard for that kind of a tab.

Most of the eating establishments in this book are cafes. But we have also included what we have termed "country restaurants." In our minds, a country restaurant is one that generally but not necessarily focuses on a narrow range of food—say, fried chicken and catfish served family-style. Another way the two might be distinguished is that a country restaurant is apt to be grander in scale, such as Harold's Country Kitchen in Donna or Sartin's in Sabine Pass.

We did not feel it necessary to have an equal geographic balance in this book. Obviously, a good cafe is where you find it; we can't help that. So as it turned out, we included more cafes and country restaurants from the eastern side of Texas than the western half. As I have said, that was purely a function of quality rather than anything else.

Since the cafes and country restaurants mentioned in this book are independent businesses run by some very independent people, it is possible that the hours, prices, decor, or menu might have changed by the time you visit. Don't despair. You can write your book next.

As I grow older, Texas seems to keep changing. Don't misunderstand me; I'm not opposed to change. It doesn't bother me that gas stations don't check your oil and your air or even pump your gas. I don't care that there are hardly any dime stores or barbershops or drive-in movie theaters that show something besides pornography. Those aren't the things that define our state. But cafes are different, and their waning numbers underscore the erosions of old Texas. The day may come when the only Texas cafe you'll be able to find will be in Fort Worth's Amon Carter Museum—and it won't serve food.

This erosion didn't start yesterday, of course; it's been happening for years. Obviously it has something to do with the development of the Interstate Highway system, which avoids small towns, and with the growth of fast-food chains. How can a local cafe survive a highway bypass or compete with the marketing macho of McDonald's, Wendy's, Dairy Queen, or Sonic? Still, the cafe hasn't vanished altogether. If you look hard enough, you can still find authentic Texas cafes. You just have to know where to look, and unfortunately for urbanites, the city is usually not the place (though there are a few notable exceptions). To find the real thing you have to search in small towns, and you have to get off the freeways.

Once you've discovered what appears to be a cafe, you need to check it for authenticity. A simple but generally reliable rule is that real cafes usually call themselves "cafes." Another good test is the cashier's counter. A glass display case with a well-worn cash register and a spindle holding plenty of "Dining Out Is Fun" receipts is a promising sign. Another is the local club placard. If the Lions eat there, it's probably good enough for you.

Speaking of signs, an authentic cafe has lots of them. At Orsak's Cafe in Fayetteville, you'll find this pearl of wisdom: "Don't criticize your wife, remember who she married." At another place we noted that "Spending money can seriously damage your wealth." Cafe owners also post a lot of rules on hand-lettered signs, mostly having to do with intoxication on the premises, bounced checks, and a minimum dress code, as in "No shoes, no shirt, no service." We're glad to see that "We reserve the right to refuse service to anyone" has all but disappeared from the walls of Texas cafes.

The strangest "Hours Open" sign we found was at Michalsky's Cafe in Fayetteville: "Open as long as there is a light. No light, no open." Below it in smaller, handwritten letters is written, "Cooks gone dancing." We were told that the sign was made by one of the owner's good friends, now deceased—gone, we hope, to that ultimate honky-tonk.

Because cafe owners have to spend so much time in their places of business, they personalize their surroundings. We haven't seen one cafe in Texas that didn't have a photograph or two on the walls, most often of children and grandchildren. Tied for second are photographs of high school cheerleaders and of sportsmen proudly displaying trophy deer or fish. Should you want the cafe owner to talk to you instead of just ringing up your tab, ask about the pictures.

One of the admirable things about the people who own cafes is that they all seem to possess an attitude of "Make do with what you have got, then you'll have no need for what you have not." Sarah's Cafe in Fort Stockton marks its ladies' room with a picture of a woman cut from a magazine—no words, no universal gender symbols, just straightforward graphic communication. That same make-do attitude is likely the reason you never see cafe employees wearing uniforms. If you do, the cafe has probably been recently purchased by a yuppie drop-out who still drives a BMW. Please, turn on your heel and exit.

Cafe menus aren't fancy, and they're invariably used until they wear out. You're bound to see a lot of prices that have been changed, new items scribbled in, old ones inked out. Our favorite menus are the ones with generic pictures made by V. C. Menus in Eastland. On one trip across Texas we once saw the same picture of a hamburger at three different places in a single day. The most sensible menu for a cafe is a chalkboard, which conveys a sense of just-cooked food and never leaves you wondering why they raised the price of catfish from $3.55 to $3.65.

We like cafes for all the condiments and food accessories that let the customers do it their way. Is the meat loaf not quite to your taste? Never fear. Right at your fingertips are salt, pepper, A.1. Steak Sauce, mustard, catsup, Worcestershire sauce, Tabasco, Evangeline Red Hot Sauce, ReaLemon, sugar, Sweet 'N Low, Cremora, margarine, and one of those narrow-necked bottles of vinegar with lots of little green peppers in it.

You can find wonderful, quirky things for sale in cafes, too. The Farmer's Market Cafe in El Paso displays an ad for getting your baby's shoes bronzed with Senti-Metal. Sarah's Cafe in Fort Stockton will sell you bubble gum in the shape of tacos. And the New Ulm Tavern and Cafe in New Ulm sells more packaged junk food than you ever knew existed.

Though cafes have a lot in common, no two are exactly alike. America's fear of the unknown has let many restaurants, fast-food places in particular, cash in on predictability while treating food as something less than vital. A Texas cafe, luckily, is a place where food is still more important than style or speed. Cafe eating is honest, no-frills eating. It's also a real bargain. Where else can you buy a hand-breaded chicken-fried steak with a fresh green salad, homemade french fries, and a vegetable or two for only $3.50?

Cafe owners work fifteen hours a day, cope with the ever-changing price of goods while keeping menu prices stable, and get up at five in the morning so that you and I might eat our two fried eggs at seven. As long as people are still willing to work that hard for that little, let's enjoy the cafes that remain.

Finally—and this will come as no surprise to you—Texas is a big state. Big enough, in fact, that cafes and cafe menus vary by region. In East Texas, cafes seem to specialize in chicken-fried steak, fresh Gulf seafood, and homemade bread and pies. In the Hill Country, by contrast, where one finds a lot of German, Czech, and Polish settlements, cafe menus feature such items as kolaches, sauerkraut, and sausages. In West Texas, most cafes and country restaurants reflect the strong influence of nearby Mexico with such items as enchiladas, tacos, refried beans, and specialties such as *cabrito*.

Wherever in Texas you travel, we hope that this book will help you enjoy beyond the obvious. With it, you'll have some alternatives to the fast-food chains that we all know and use occasionally. Keep this book in your car, because when you're driving far from home, that's when you'll need it most.

To all of our readers, good luck. And may the best chicken-fried steak win.

Panhandle

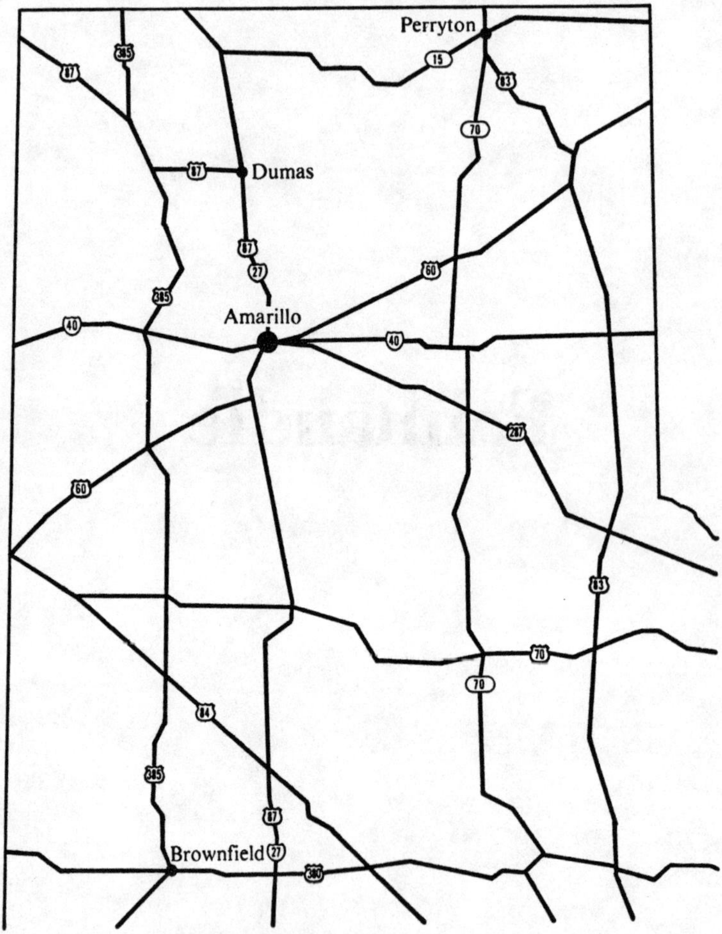
Perryton
15
385
87
83
70
Dumas
87
87
27
60
385
Amarillo
40
40
287
60
83
70
70
84
385
87
Brownfield
27
380

Amarillo

BLUE FRONT CAFE

*F*or thirty-five years the Blue Front Cafe operated at 821 W. 6th, a block west of the new location. "The building literally wore out," new owner Betty Malson relates. "The concrete was worn thin from the years the customers had tread on it, and the plumbing was gone." But with kid-glove handling, which included personal conversations with the customers and many tours of their new dining surroundings, the successful transition has been made. "After all, it isn't really the building that made the Blue Front so special, it was and still is the satisfied customers served during lunch and the good food they're served." These satisfied customers (some who have been coming in for more than thirty years) are from all walks of life. Betty says, "They come here to eat and mingle with one another in an amiable atmosphere, then leave to go back to their individual situations. But at least while they are here they are treated like a special person."

The Blue Front Cafe is also synonymous with fast service—so much so that in the summer of 1984, a German film crew for a program much like our *60 Minutes* filmed a documentary about the Blue Front's efficiency for German television. The Blue Front can serve 150 at lunch. Diners are served with friendliness but at a supersonic pace. This doesn't mean you'll get whiplash while eating, but if you need to get going, you can.

The reputation of the awesome fast service comes from career waitresses such as Mae Smith (twenty-seven years of experience) and Lorene Ballard (fourteen years). They set the pace and keep it for the rest of the staff.

Lunch specials Monday through Friday are beef tips, enchiladas, fried chicken, meat loaf, and pork ribs. A unique sandwich is the Porker Delight—chopped pork on a bun served with a secret sauce. A Curley-Q-Tater goes with it. (That's a fried sliced potato in one continuous piece that looks like a pig's tail.) All for $1.65.

Get off the interstate, stop awhile, dine with the regulars such as Amarillo Slim (a famous gambler in these parts), city councilmen, doctors, mechanics, and even the mayor. "No one needs to leave these doors unsatisfied," Betty told us. You won't.

801 W. 6th
(806) 372-0659
Monday–Friday 6 a.m.–4 p.m.
Saturday 6 a.m.–2 p.m.

STOCKYARDS CAFE

*T*his establishment is not easy to find. It's situated on the northeast side of Amarillo, far from the main thoroughfare and residential areas but next to the railroad tracks. Where? Are you lost? Ask any gas-station attendant, because for twenty-five years this restaurant has been serving the best breakfast and steak lunches with prices that seem to be frozen in time.

Complete with pickup trucks, the parking lot sets the atmosphere. Inside the entry, through the door to the left, is the stark-walled cafe. The decor consists of authentic cowboys with their spurs and chaps rapidly filling up this 140-seat capacity eatery.

Hearty breakfasts of eggs; sausage, bacon, or ham; hash browns;

biscuits with gravy; and coffee, all for $2.55, are served all morning. The most popular eating here, though, is steak. The "Republican Club with Democratic Flavor" seems to please everybody. It is an eight-ounce cut of top sirloin served with homemade french fries, green tossed salad, homemade yeast rolls, and tea, for $5.35. There are rib eyes, T-bones, and strips, too, for $6.75. If steak is not your preference, you can eat from the buffet, where you have a choice of five meats (hamburger steak, chicken-fried steak, roast beef, short ribs, and meat loaf), eight to ten vegetables (canned, fresh, or frozen), homemade rolls, and a drink, for $3.50. Gilbert Jeffers and his son Gilbert (there is a junior here somewhere) cut their own meat daily. The puddings are homemade, and rolls are made daily. A hundred pounds of potatoes are peeled each morning for hash browns, french fries, and mashed potatoes.

We didn't forget. The door to the right in the entry leads to the stockyards.

3rd and Manhattan
Amarillo Livestock Auction
Building
(806) 373-1591
Monday—Saturday 6 a.m.—2 p.m.

Brownfield

KOUNTRY KITCHEN

*C*harlotte Wilkes is not a new cafe owner, just operating in a new location. When we talked with her she said she "was still getting organized" after having opened her doors only the day before. But the word "disorganized" never crossed our minds; rather, we had complete confidence in Charlotte. The homemade cinnamon rolls for 75¢ and fresh-brewed coffee hit the spot. We could have had homemade cherry turnovers at 75¢, too. And while breakfast was a lazy affair for us, we could tell that preparations for lunch were not. Homemade fillings of chicken, tuna, and pimiento cheese were being made for sandwiches—which are served, by the way, on slices of bread made on the premises. The day's lunch special of roast beef with brown gravy, mashed potatoes, and tossed salad for $4.95 was being put together, too. Charlotte also told us of the Kountry Kitchen's cheese enchilada casserole, which "draws them in from all over the South Plains." It is one of her favorite recipes, and she shares it with her customers. Texas cream pie is the house specialty dessert, for $1 a slice. Another exceptional item is cream cheese brownies at 60¢ each.

The warmth of the Kountry Kitchen emanates from the helpful waitresses, friendly local folks dining there, and the country decor. Be sure to review Charlotte's plate collection; it tells you in what month you're eating.

1202 Lubbock
(806) 637-8268
Monday–Wednesday, Friday 7:30 a.m.–3 p.m.
Thursday 7:30–3, 6 p.m.–8:30 p.m. (steak night)

PLAZA RESTAURANT

*T*his is the only Texas cafe that we know about where you can get fried quail for breakfast. The Plaza Restaurant has been around for more than thirty years and has been run by one Crowder or another for all that time. It was started by ex-farmers Doyle and Lou Crowder. Now the day-to-day operation is squarely on the shoulders of son Eddie Crowder.

For breakfast, for $3.49, you can get fried quail, two eggs, hash browns, hot biscuits, and gravy. The menu offers some seventy-five items from which to choose, including steaks, Mexican food, fifteen different sandwiches, chicken-fried steak, and country sausage.

At lunch, specials change daily, but they might include meat loaf or barbecued beef tips as well as seven other choices. Specials come with green salad, a vegetable, lima beans, hot rolls, and cornbread, all for $3.95. Even though the Gulf is not exactly nearby, you can get stuffed crabs and fried oysters, too.

If you find yourself hungry and you're heading into Texas from New Mexico or out of Texas to New Mexico, come by the Plaza Restaurant. It's a good pit stop.

1312 W. Main
(806) 637-3904
Tuesday–Sunday 6 a.m.–9 p.m.

Dumas

CHARRED OAK RESTAURANT

*T*he Charred Oak Restaurant is a steak house. But we figure that if you're driving in the High Plains of Texas and you're hungry, you'd better eat a good meal wherever and whenever. Pickin's are slim up here. Betty Hodges, owner of the Charred Oak, says, "Dumas needed this type of restaurant. We serve quality food at a fair price."

If you're eating a light lunch, try their homemade chicken salad, Mexican salad, or hamburgers made with fresh ground beef served on a grilled bun. Or you can meander over to the chockablock salad bar. Heap your plate with choices of freshly made taco, mushroom, corn, pasta, potato, or vegetable salads and condiments like green onions, cherry tomatoes, pickled beets, okra, and more. You can counter all these low-calorie foods by being sure to eat several of their homemade yeast rolls. All this gluttony will set you back $5.95. And don't pass up the chocolate mousse; a fruit salad is available, but a lot of it is canned.

The heavier entrées for lunch vary every day; you'll have either steak fingers, marinated steak bits served on a bed of rice, popcorn shrimp, hamburger steak, or catfish, served with french fries, a baked potato, or fried (frozen) okra, all for $4.75. At night, Betty says, "We serve the best prime rib in the country. That's what many, many of our customers tell us." The other favorites are "calf fries" (better known to us as "mountain oysters"), served on Thursday evenings, and chicken-fried steak, served on Tuesdays. The chicken-fried is a generous portion of tenderized beef, covered with cream gravy, griddle-fried, and served with a potato and a trip to the salad bar. The decor is authentic western. All those brands on the walls were burnt in by the "who's who" ranchers in the Dumas area.

1521 S. Dumas
(806) 935-7664
Monday—Friday 11 a.m.—9 p.m.
Saturday 5 p.m.—9 p.m.

Perryton

DUTCH INN

With a buffet line that offers twelve salads, four meats, eight vegetables, homemade rolls, and a fresh-daily fruit cobbler for dessert, you no longer have to speculate about why customers dutifully line up outside for more than a block waiting to eat. They anticipate making their food selections from salads made from scratch. Choices range from Heavenly Hash, Apricot Delight, or Waldorf salad to an array of Jello salads, potato salad, or coleslaw. They know they also have the opportunity to choose from meat dishes such as baked turkey, roast beef, fried chicken, pork chops, big pure beef franks, Polish sausage, or pit barbecue. And then there are the vegetable dishes: Italian-style green beans, beets, corn, and sweet potatoes, to name a few. All of this costs $4.25 during the week and $4.75 on Sundays. Dessert and fresh-brewed tea or coffee are included.

These dishes are prepared by several different cooks, including a salad cook who has a tenure of seventeen years, a bakery cook, and a dinner cook. "For more than twenty-two years," owner Lewis Andrews remarks, "we have specialized in home cooking. Our efforts have made us famous with people in these parts. We don't make a lot of money, but we sure have good friends."

For early morning crowds, there is a breakfast cook on hand, too, whipping up bacon, ham, or sausage, two eggs, homemade hash browns, grits, homemade biscuits, and cream gravy, with all the coffee you can drink, for $3.19. The amount of coffee served is a tell-tale sign of the popularity of this spot. Every morning by ten o'clock, 100 gallons of coffee have been swallowed. Lewis exclaims, "Be sure to tell 'em there are no waffles served after 10 a.m. Folks love those waffles."

711 N. Main
(806) 435-3471
Open seven days, 6 a.m.—10 p.m.

North/Northeast

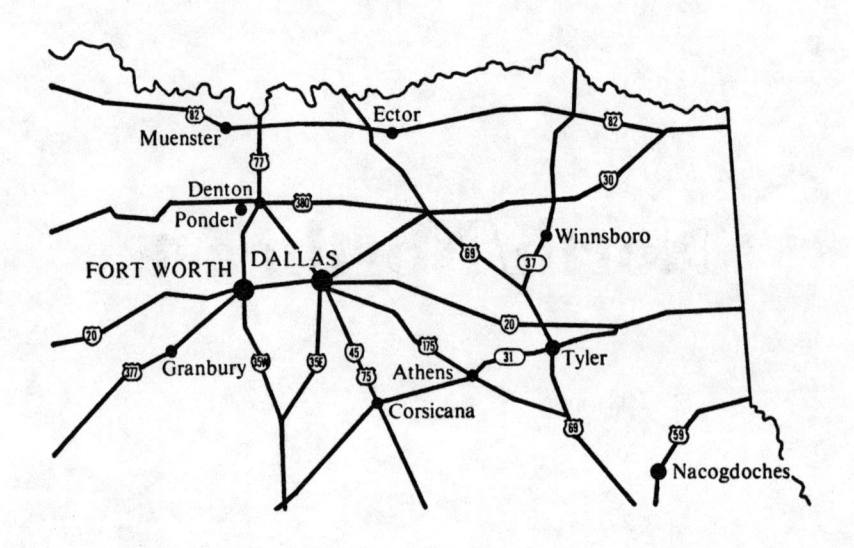

Athens

MAY'S CAFE

*I*n the Coon Creek area between Athens and Palestine, seventy-eight-year-old May Martin has been serving some of the best country food around for fifty-three years. Her customers are construction workers, farmers, fishermen, and even celebrities such as Willie Nelson, Waylon Jennings, and Hank Williams, Jr. Like many cafes in deep East Texas, May's is a little rough-and-tumble—perhaps not the place to bring your stuffy Aunt Flossie. Even so, it has a certain charm: each table (and there are only seven) has a centerpiece of fresh onions and green jalapeño and serrano peppers. Cows graze in a pasture nearby, and from the window you can watch wild birds chowing down the cafe's day-old hushpuppies.

For human customers, there's roast beef, chicken-fried steak, and barbecued ham. (All the barbecuing is done on an old A&M barbecue pit in the smokehouse, and about fifty pounds of meat is cooked there every other day.) On Thursday May buys fresh vegetables from Dallas. For dessert you can choose from several kinds of homemade cobbler—apple, peach, and berry, to mention three. An entire meal, including cobbler, is $4.

US Hwy. 19 (6 mi. south)
No phone
Wednesday—Monday 5:30 a.m.—5 p.m.

Corsicana

ROY'S CAFE

When Vernon McGuyer came to Corsicana in 1976, he had only $128 in his pocket. Today he owns and runs Roy's Cafe, which feeds around five hundred people a day. Checking the company logos on customers' shirts, we noted Sears, Pinkerton's, Mrs. Baird's Bread, the local Cadillac dealership, and a pipeline company. The phone keeps ringing because members of the cafe's elite are often paged while on their coffee breaks.

Roy's is a friendly, energetic place that serves all the coffee you can drink for the price of one cup. All told, the eight veterans among the employees have put in more than 140 years at the cafe.

After examining the business cards and memorabilia on the bulletin board, visitors should try the homemade biscuits or the cinnamon toast (cinnamon on both sides and topped with more sugar than your mother ever allowed).

306 N. Beaton
(214) 874-6791
Monday–Saturday 5 a.m.–3 p.m.

Denton

BRIAR INN

*E*leven years ago Marvin Wynn's Briar Inn could seat a total of nineteen people—eleven at stools along the counter and the rest at two booths. Now the cafe has room for ninety-six. The only way a cafe can experience growth is by serving good food, and you can believe the Briar Inn's menu when you read, "House of fine food—quality is our specialty."

Marvin had good training. His father, Lem Railsback (of the Railsback Cafe in Fort Stockton), taught him a lot. Marvin says, "I used to sit for hours and talk to Dad while he cooked. I would watch his techniques, and I guess some of them did rub off on me."

Being so far from Fort Stockton, we're in luck. At breakfast Marvin uses Lem's recipe for pancakes—you can get 'em here, too! A stack (three is a stack, in case you didn't know) is $1.80. Or you can try one of Marvin's special omelettes. He guarantees, "It'll be one of the best you've even eaten."

Of course, there is chicken-fried steak—a fresh beef cutlet dipped in flour, egg, and milk then floured again (just like Lem's), griddle-fried, served with pan cream gravy and your choice of homemade french fries, hash browns, or baked potato. (Those 600 pounds of potatoes Marvin buys a week are going somewhere!) It's served with a green salad with your choice of dressing—all the quality you could want for $5.50.

A popular menu item is the Briar Inn's hand-rolled enchiladas. Marvin takes fresh tortillas and fills them with freshly grated longhorn cheddar cheese and grated onions, rolls them up, and tops them with homemade sauce and then more cheddar cheese. Then they're baked. This scrumptious dish is presented to you with a portion of lettuce and tomato, a green onion, and a jalapeño pepper. You get three to an order for $5.50. Burger Bill of Denton says they have the best hamburgers in these parts; we'll take his word for it. We have to have some choices for our next visit.

3620 S. IH 35—Denton State School exit
(817) 387-7616
Monday–Friday 6 a.m.–10 p.m.
Saturday 6 a.m.–3 p.m.

TOM AND JO'S CAFE

*R*emember those places that used to have individual jukebox selectors in every booth? Tom and Jo's Cafe is one of them; you slide into your booth, punch up Willie Nelson singing "Mamas, Don't Let Your Babies Grow Up To Be Cowboys"; order; and never miss a bite or a beat. All in all, Tom and Jo's is a pretty decent cafe; nothing is outstanding, but nothing is really bad, either. After eating at plenty of places where nothing was really good, we've come to respect proprietors like Gerald Sitton, who gives you a palatable meal at an honest price. A good cheeseburger in a basket, served with real french fries, is $2.45. A slice of homemade pie is 95¢. Tom and Jo's also has lunch specials, but avoid the vegetables unless you like them canned.

702 S. Elm
(817) 382-8314
Monday—Saturday 6 a.m.—8 p.m.

Ector

FEED MILL

*E*ctor, a farm community of 573 people, boasts a restaurant called the Feed Mill, which serves some of the best chicken-fried steak in the state of Texas, described by *Texas Monthly* in its 1980 "Best" list as "large, tender, country-spiced, and cream-gravied." How could you even think of not stopping in? Dolly and Carl Stone, transplanted New Yorkers, have been serving as a team since 1979. Carl drives an eighteen-wheeler for a fertilizer company a lot of the time. Dolly says of their cafe business, "I raised and fed four sons. I knew I could do this, too."

The menu is not just meat and potatoes. The Feed Mill also dishes up chicken-fried steak, hamburgers, T-bones, rib eyes, fried shrimp, fried oysters, roast beef, quail, and Mexican food dishes. There's also a salad bar. The most popular daily special is the acclaimed chicken-fried steak, served with homemade gravy, french fries, coleslaw, Texas toast, and tea or coffee, for $3.95. If there is room, and you should save some, Dolly has slices of homemade chocolate, coconut, and apple pies to choose from for 70¢ a serving.

On Sundays you have a choice of chicken-fried steak, steak fingers, or chicken strips, served with french fries, baked potato, or potatoes *au gratin* and vegetable choices of coleslaw, green beans, corn, fried okra, or squash. Dinner rolls and tea or coffee complete the meal, all for $3.95. (Too bad Sunday comes but once a week!)

The decor of the Feed Mill is as varied as the menu. A feed mill is exactly what the restaurant was in the early 1900s, and today the tables and chairs are actually placed on the old platform scales where trucks and wagons had their loads weighed out. The walls are decorated with feed bags, horse yokes, old advertising feed signs, muleshoes, and black-and-white photos of Ector as it was in the 1950s.

Dolly has a guest book with the signatures of visitors from all over the world. Of course, her customers also include Ector locals—even school children during the lunch crunch and North Texas residents and hungry folks who come by for the first time.

201 N. Main
(214) 961-3355
Tuesday—Saturday 10 a.m.—8 p.m.
Sunday 11:30 a.m.—3 p.m.

Granbury

NUTT HOUSE

*I*t all began with two blind brothers—Jesse and Jacob Nutt. They opened a store in 1886 selling general merchandise to neighboring settlers. As was the tradition back then, the Nutt brothers often put up travelers overnight in their own homes. As this tradition intensified, so too did the need for a real hotel, so in 1919 the Nutt brothers built the structure you see today.

The upstairs still functions as a hotel with ten rooms, and the nearby annex has five more. Prices range from $25 for a room to $85 for a suite. In the original hotel you'll have to share the "water closet," so be prepared. There are no phones or televisions, but believe it or not, reservations are a must. That has a lot to do with the Granbury Opera House, which draws a heavy crowd from Dallas and Fort Worth.

Granbury is basically a restored turn-of-the-century little town. One might easily describe it as bordering on being a tourist trap. There are more than twenty antiques stores, and busloads of tourists arrive here on weekends and weekdays for a bit of nostalgia.

That's where the Nutt House comes back into play. In the downstairs dining room you can pretty much depend on a solid country-style buffet lunch or dinner. Young women in old-style long dresses will pour you coffee or tea. In the buffet line you can choose from two meats, a choice of fresh vegetables, salads with homemade dressings, and their famous hot-water cornbread. We had their buttermilk pie for dessert, for which they are famous, too. They also serve a good peach cobbler. Lunch buffet costs $4.95, and dinner will run you $6.95. Next door is a terrific candy store for homemade fudge.

The Nutt House is now owned by Tony Dauphinot and managed by Madge Peters. What the Nutt House is all about is dining down memory lane, and if you can stand such an obvious display of corn, you'll love the food.

On the square
(817) 573-9362
Tuesday—Thursday 11:30 a.m.—2 p.m.
Friday and Saturday 11:30—2 and 6 p.m.—8 p.m.
Sunday 11:30 a.m.—3 p.m.

NUTT SHELL

*E*ven though co-owner Barbara Stevenson says, "I'm a blithering idiot after five years of this," we sense she's at least a happy blithering idiot. The Nutt Shell is no longer a tiny drop-in eatery sitting in the Nutt House's shadow. After five years of hard work, Barbara Stevenson and Kay Collerain have established a cafe and a bakery that has earned statewide recognition.

For example, the hamburgers were deemed the best by *D* magazine. Fresh ground meat nestled in an on-the-premises-bakery-baked cracked-wheat bun served with potato chips and dill pickles is $2.95. The Killer, which is very popular, is a three-quarter-pound double meat, double cheese, avocado, and bacon burger served with potato chips and dill pickles for $4.95. Every day there are also blue plate specials; you might choose from chicken-fried steak, Mom's pot roast, meat loaf, smothered steak, or fried fish, served with fresh vegetables, homemade rolls and bread, and homemade desserts (apple cobbler, bread pudding, and cherry pie, to name a few), all for $3.65.

Or maybe you'd prefer a four-ounce scoop of Texas's own Blue Bell ice cream packed into a homemade cone. Cones are made from scratch—no mixes here.

On a blistering hot Texas day, the best thirst remedy is the Nutt Shell's fresh-squeezed lemonade for $1 a glass. Your taste buds will cry for joy.

On the square
(817) 573-6261
Open seven days, 9 a.m.—5 p.m.

Muenster

ROHMER'S

At one time, riverbeds were scooped out and their bountiful regurgitation of stone was used by pioneer German builders for homes. Rohmer's is located in a house such as that. This little converted dwelling without decor serves up to ninety local businessmen, farmers, oil operators, and sundry Muensterites at a time. The workingman's meal includes frog legs, steaks, fried chicken, barbecue, chicken-fried steak, and Mexican food dishes. "Sometimes we serve German food," owner Emil Rohmer says, "but people here are mostly tired of it since this is a strong German settlement." And since Emil has owned this restaurant for more than thirty-one years, you respect his judgment. "About once a month we'll do hot German potato salad with sauerkraut and German sausages." We were disappointed it wasn't that time. But Mrs. Rohmer's fabulous cheesecake quickly brought us appeasement. There are three to choose from: chocolate amaretto, pecan praline, and New York, each $1.50 a slice. Every bite was as flavorful and creamy as the last.

US Hwy. 82
(817) 759-2973
Monday—Thursday 6:30 a.m.—10 p.m.
Friday and Saturday 6:30 a.m.—11 p.m.

Nacogdoches

CHEF LATIN'S

*A*lison Cook, an editor of *Texas Monthly* magazine, awarded Chef Latin's the distinction of having the best mashed potatoes in Texas. We agree. We also think their chicken-fried steak with cream gravy would rate high if there were a statewide contest, not to mention their homemade cornbread, which you personally get to slather with butter. Another contender is the chicken strips, served with vegetables, mashed potatoes, cream gravy, and tossed green salad ($4.25). The vegetable might be seasonally fresh or "fixed-up" canned. The man in charge of all this, Arthur Latin, was formerly a chef at Annie's Kitchen for ten years. In 1982 he moved his expertise into the building that was once occupied by Hines Cafe. He moved the pool tables out, making space for eight more tables.

In the old pool table room and the main dining area, the Rolls-Royce crowd from Dallas, Fort Worth, and Houston fill their plates with mouth-watering morsels. "We cook just like we cook at home," says Arthur. Sometimes, "when we get the notion to do that," Arthur offers off-the-menu items such as barbecue brisket, ribs, and chicken, served with potato salad and baked beans made from scratch and seasoned with bacon and onions. He also serves grilled twelve-ounce rib eye steaks for $7.95.

118 Shawnee
(409) 560-4420
Monday–Thursday, Sunday 11 a.m.–8 p.m.
Friday and Saturday 11 a.m.–10 p.m.

Ponder

RANCHMAN'S CAFE

"*W*hy don't you to go Ponder/ And tear a steak asunder/Then you too will cease to wonder/Why we all go oft' to Ponder." This verse, the first poetry we have ever encountered that was inspired by a steak, was written in the guest book at Ranchman's by a satisfied customer. By way of explanation, owner Grace "Pete" Jackson says modestly, "We just cook like we cook at home."

So famous is this place that Hugh O'Brien, Ruth Buzzie, Lindsay Wagner, and visitors from London, Paris, and Puerto Rico have signed the guest book with raves. Some guests insist on having a souvenir. President Jimmy Carter's mother, Miss Lillian, purchased the cafe's rustic outhouse several years ago and had it delivered to her daughter's home in nearby Argyle.

The reason for Ranchman's popularity is clear. Pete cuts her own thick, juicy steaks exclusively from the short loin and loin end, reserving the trimming to be ground up into some of the best hamburger meat in North Texas. Lunch specials change daily, and breakfast always includes cured ham or bacon. Lunches are $3.95, steaks $7.75 and up. To top it all off, Pete makes some of the best pies in the state, using only fresh ingredients. A pie like her chocolate—made from real chocolate, not a pudding mix—is a rarity in cafes. Knowledgeable customers reserve slices before they sit down to eat, and they also make reservations to dine. Given the atmosphere, the food, the one-block downtown in which the cafe is located, and the personality of Pete herself, Ranchman's has everything you could ask for in a cafe.

Bailey St. 1/2 block west of FM Rd. 156
(Across from the post office)
(817) 479-2221
Open seven days 11:30 a.m.–10 p.m.

Tyler

RUNNING W RESTAURANT

*O*wner Tom Waddell says that this 60-by-100-foot white metal building is "nothing fancy." But Tom and his wife Eliuth know their way around the kitchen. "We fix it right or it doesn't go out." Their barbecue is hickory smoked and done on the premises. A barbecue plate has pinto beans, coleslaw, Texas toast, jalapeño peppers, and home french fries or a baked potato, all for $5.95. There are hamburgers, too, made with a quarter-pound of meat ground fresh daily (not processed), as well as T-bones and rib eyes. "We try to use the best meat." They also serve chicken-fried steak—a five-ounce patty, covered with cream or brown gravy, and served with home-style french fries, salad from the salad bar, and Texas toast for $4.99. The big golden fried onion rings are Eliuth's specialty. Don't eat all the available homemade bread because you'll need to leave room to try 'em.

A very rare handmade cotton-gin scale sits in the east end of the room. The whole apparatus can be taken apart by hand and stored in a compact manner. Give it a gander. Oh, that thirteen-foot snakeskin is not representative of the rattlesnakes in these parts; that's a boa skin. But that's another story.

IH 20—Willowbranch exit (544)
(214) 963-8974
Open seven days, 24 hours

Winnsboro

LOU'S COUNTRY INN

We couldn't help but question Becky Hightower about why Lou's Country Inn is closed during Saturday lunches. In the cafe world, Saturdays are usually pretty good business days. Becky's retort was, "We get tired. We need to rest. We make everything here from scratch, the hard way!" She laughs, "Lou and I [Lou Murley is a woman and part-owner] started this cafe as a hobby. We had raised our mutual families of four children each and wanted something to fill the void. So we started this cafe, and it has turned into a much bigger business than we ever expected."

It's easy to see why, and the more than a hundred people they serve at lunch serve as a testimonial. The lunch buffet choices will have you stymied as to what to try. Roast beef, chicken-fried steak, baked chicken dishes, and fried chicken are a few of the meat dishes offered. They put out fresh East Texas vegetables and fruits—so fresh, in fact, that farmers deliver their goods to the door. Sometimes Becky and Lou's menu has zucchini, sweet potatoes (sweet potato pie), black-eyed peas, or green beans to sample. Seven salads are usually available—green pea salad, pasta, rice, and Jello salads, to name a few. All for $4.50.

If you want to eat lighter, try their soup and sandwich special for $3.95. The soup might be fresh mushroom, spicy tomato, clam chowder, or cream of fresh asparagus; but whatever is served, all the soups are made fresh daily. The sandwiches are chicken salad, pimiento cheese, and tunafish, all served on homemade whole wheat bread.

The good food is complemented by pleasant surroundings. Lou's Country Inn is really a 1900s Victorian restored home, painted Cape Cod blue and decorated in early American antiques. Local artists have adorned the walls with oil and watercolor paintings. If you are particularly fond of one, ask about it; it might be for sale.

Texas Hwy. 37 (2 mi. south)
(214) 629-7199
Tuesday—Friday, Sunday 11 a.m.—2 p.m.

Central

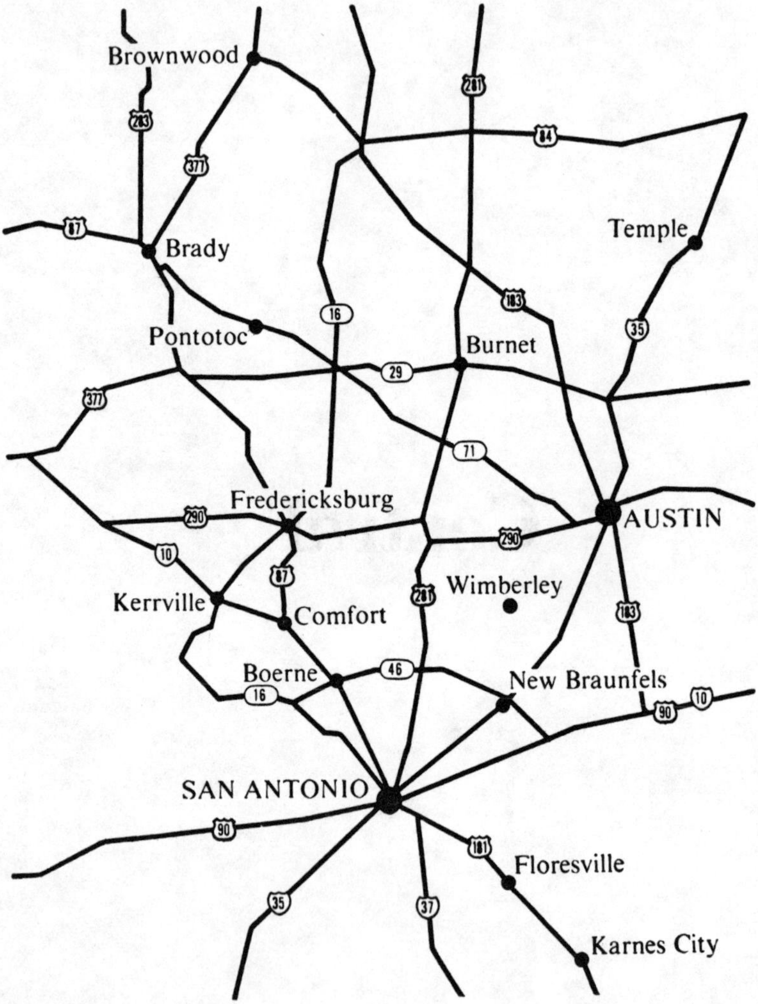
Brownwood
283
377
87
Brady
Pontotoc
16
281
84
Temple
183
35
Burnet
29
377
71
Fredericksburg
AUSTIN
290
290
10
87
281
Wimberley
183
Kerrville
Comfort
Boerne
46
16
New Braunfels
90
10
SAN ANTONIO
90
181
Floresville
35
37
Karnes City

Boerne

COUNTRY SPIRIT

*T*his cafe was described as "a family operation, even though we're really not related," by manager Eva Sanderson. Housed in an a pre–Civil War two-story home with a seemingly endless ceiling, the structure has wooden floors and is painted a fresh blue. The menu consists of country fixin's with a shade of city knowledge. We tried the sautéed chicken strips—chicken rolled in bread crumbs, browned in butter, and served with a choice of waffle fries, a baked potato, or "house" rice, a standard salad, and potato rolls from their own recipe for a mere $6.95. This is cook Little Joe's recipe. If you have a tad of Spanish in your vocabulary you know why they are no longer served as "Little Joe's Pelotas."

All desserts are homemade: margarita pie, cheesecake, pecan pies, bread pudding, and chocolate cake. When you find yourself hungry between Comfort and Bandera, this is a primo choice.

707 S. Main
(512) 249-3607
Monday, Wednesday, Sunday 11 a.m.–9 p.m.
Friday and Saturday 11 a.m.–10 p.m.

Brady

CLUB CAFE

*T*he Art Deco—inspired building that houses the twenty-year-old Club Cafe cuts a sharp contrast to the pickup trucks in the parking lot. On the inside, the entire cafe is carpeted with sculpted wall-to-wall pile in a trendy khaki color. The booths have been separated with posts, like horse stalls, and on the walls are framed photographs from Brady's local paper—a girl's tap dance recital, some Shetland ponies, a man who has caught a three-foot catfish.

Travelers, ranchers, businessmen, and preachers stop by for the Texas-size cinnamon rolls and glazed doughnuts made fresh each morning. Every table has five or six empty coffee mugs at the ready, to be filled instantly as waitresses work the floor. With breakfast everyone gets homemade biscuits and a bowl of smooth cream gravy. Initially doubtful, we found ourselves eating "gravy biscuits" with wild abandon after one taste. An order consisting of one egg over easy, hash browns (regrettably the frozen variety), instant hot chocolate, and those terrific biscuits and gravy costs about $2.50.

The cafe is definitely worth a Friday-night dinner as well, when you can get fried catfish, home-sliced french fries or a baked potato,

homemade hushpuppies, and a trip to the salad bar, for just $4.50.
We hear that the cafe fries more than two hundred pounds of catfish every week. Fayrene Parks is the owner.

506 Commerce (US Hwy. 87)
(915) 597-7522
Open seven days, 5:30 a.m.–10 p.m.

Brownwood

UNDERWOOD'S CAFETERIA

*U*nderwood's Cafeteria and succulent barbecue are synonymous. Leonard Underwood boasts proudly, "If you say Brownwood in these parts, people say, that's where Underwood's is"—and has been for more than thirty-five years. At one time there were Underwood's in Amarillo, Wichita Falls, and Lubbock, but now you have to go Brownwood to enjoy their famous food. Every day you can enjoy barbecue beef, steaks, chicken, German sausage, spare ribs, or Momma's fried chicken. The daily special meats in the cafeteria line include chicken-fried steak, fried shrimp, freshwater catfish, and barbecued ham. It's "an all you can eat, except for the meat" proposition that comes with an array of vegetables (some fresh, mostly canned), salads, and fresh-brewed tea or coffee and a homemade dessert for $5.25. There are homemade yeast rolls straight from the oven, and the house specialty dessert is peach cobbler. "We want to please our customers," Leonard confides. With standards that are as high as his, we predict they will continue to do just that for another thirty-five years.

404 W. Commerce
(915) 646-6110
Thursday–Tuesday 9 a.m.–9 p.m.

Burnet

BLUE BONNET CAFE

*T*he white stucco 1930s-style building is quiet most of the year, but during summer sessions at nearby Camp Longhorn, says co-owner Bonnie Marx, the walls echo with the noise of camp counselors' shenanigans. We got the idea, though, that Bonnie is happy to be overrun year after year by campers and others who come to eat some of the freshest and best fried catfish in the state.

This flaky fish, dipped in cornmeal and served with real french fries, hushpuppies, and (sorry) an unremarkable salad, comes in small and large portions for $5 and $6.25. The day we ate there it was close to perfection; our only lament was that plastic packets of ReaLemon had taken the place of lemon slices. The recipe for the hushpuppies was passed down by the original owner of the Blue Bonnet, Peanut Davis.

In the dessert category, the cafe's meringue pies have become a legend in their own time; once Bonnie had to make twenty-nine in two days. But we found the 22-Minute Cake, a rich chocolate cake covered with a chocolate glaze and topped with pecans, even better. Bonnie makes it when she feels like it, so you just have to hope she feels like it on the day you visit. Celebrity advisory: Charley Pride and Faron Young have dropped in on occasion.

Texas Hwy. 29 at Buchanan Dam
8 mi. west of Burnet
No phone
Wednesday—Sunday 10 a.m.—9 p.m.
Closed three weeks at Christmas

Comfort

CYPRESS CREEK INN

*M*ost Kerrville and Fredericksburg folks are aware of this thirty-five-year-old Hill Country tradition, and you should be, too. Charlotte Holmes serves "just plain country homestyle cooking, nothing fancy" six days a week in a sprawling white building that backs up to Cypress Creek. Take a moment to admire the pecan trees on the property.

The Tuesday lunch special is baked pork chops. Wednesday's is roast-beef hash, and on Thursday there is baked ham or hamburger steak with onion gravy. On Friday you can have home-baked meat loaf, and on Saturday Mrs. Holmes serves Swiss steak with pan brown gravy. Mashed potatoes, fresh-grown vegetables of your choice, salad, a fruit juice drink, and a slice of homemade pie complete your meal, all for $3.65. The homemade pies are gastronomical experiences in themselves, with choices of peach, cherry, lemon double crust, chocolate, or coconut cream. Their crusts are still made the old-fashioned grandma way, using Gladiola flour and Snowdrift shortening.

If it's Sunday, you are in for one of Mrs. Holmes's Sunday dinner specialties. Choose from calf liver with onions, a variety of sandwiches, chef salads, fish, shrimp, or steak. During your meal ask to meet Theresa. She's been working as a waitress here for twenty-five years.

Mrs. Holmes has six grandchildren and four great-grandchildren. Her grandchildren can often be seen giving her a helping hand. Obviously, this is a family kind of place. "Don't tell 'em how old I am. I haven't given retirement a thought—as long as I have my health I'll always be here," Mrs. Holmes says with a smile.

Texas Hwy. 27
(512) 995-3977
Tuesday—Saturday 11:30 a.m.—2:30 p.m.
and 5:30—8:30 p.m.
Sunday 11:30 a.m.—2:30 p.m.

Floresville

WRIGHT'S CAFE

Wright's Cafe is the right cafe in Floresville. It is frequented by nearly everyone, including the town's most famous family, the John Connallys. An elk head belonging to John Connally's son Mark hangs here—a memento of a hunting trip to Colorado. Bert and Alma Wright started the cafe in 1954, after they did a brief stint as owners of the Baumann Cafe, also in Floresville. It was at the Baumann that they got their antique marble counter and massive stained-glass back bar. The counter case holds, besides the usual chewing tobacco and antacids, a lineup of crocheted dolls.

Bert butchers all the meat himself. The chicken-fried steak is hand-breaded, and Alma herself cuts up the chicken for frying. Most of the time you can choose from seven vegetables. Of special note for dinner is the fried quail. For dessert ask about Alma's coconut and lemon pies, which she makes from scratch when the mood strikes her. You just might be in luck. We were.

1008 C Street
(512) 393-2436
Monday—Saturday 10:30 a.m.—9:00 p.m.

Fredericksburg

HILL TOP CAFE

*D*riving out of Fredricksburg on US Hwy. 87, we were looking for the Hill Top Cafe because a satisfied customer had suggested that it had "great food and not German." Winding through the Hill Country, we thought we were lost. But on the horizon, as promised, was a radio tower and the unmistakable green and white painted roof; our car rolled to a stop in front of a sign with a greeting of "Welcome Hunters, fishermen and all other liars." We had arrived.

Brenda and Johnny Nicholas have been operating this once-isolated gas station, now-popular cafe for more than three years. They have combined Brenda's Cajun ancestry with Johnny's Greek, along with handed-down recipes from their respective families, to offer a menu that is exciting and atypical of cafe fare. A favorite weekend special is shrimp creole, for around $10.50. (Seafood is from the Gulf, so prices vary.) Or stuffed crawfish—with homemade french fries, a Greek salad, and freshly brewed iced tea to boot. A quarter-pound order of boiled cold shrimp, cooked with ingredients like cayenne pepper, crab boil, garlic, and olive oil, goes for $5.50.

Another Hill Top star is the Greek flounder. Smothered in lemon juice, garlic, a mixture of olive oil and butter, then sprinkled with parsley and grilled, it can be yours for $11.75. (Johnny's advice is to allow forty-five minutes to an hour for this.) Brenda and Johnny also serve fresh *boudin* with a side order of rice for $4.50. The Hill Top Cafe's vegetables are seasonally fresh whenever possible. Mouth-watering home-cooked desserts are available, too. I had a piece of chocolate mocha and almond cake that I am sure added yet another inch to my expanding waistline. This was $2.50. Check for daily choices.

All the seafood is fresh, brought to the Hill Top by friends who commute weekly between the bay and their country homes. Thus, the menu will change according to the catch. But you can be sure that the offerings are delectable.

Don't miss the eclectic decor. While waiting for your food, you can let your eyes wander over beer signs old and new, deer and moose heads, a Coors beer cooler, a Wurlitzer look-alike jukebox, the oak bar with brass railing, a serving tray with inlaid butterfly wings, a travel poster of Greece, and a picture representative of days gone by in Louisiana.

The piano is played on occasion by Johnny Nicholas, who can prove he hasn't lost his musical abilities from when he played with Asleep at the Wheel.

This is a popular Friday night place. Reservations should be made for parties larger than four. After eating here, you won't be amazed at how many people just sit on the outdoor patio and happily wait to be served.

US Hwy. 87
10 mi. north of Fredericksburg
(512) 997-8922
Wednesday—Saturday 11 a.m.—10 p.m.

Karnes City

POLAK'S SAWSAGE FARM

*L*et's say you are on your way to Corpus Christi from San Antonio on US Hwy. 181, and let's further say you are hungry for some country food—the kind of food you need when you're so hungry it hurts. That's when you need to stop at Polak's Sawsage Farm. Polak's is the brainchild of Al and Edna Pawelek (so now you are beginning to see where this Polish couple came up with the name for their restaurant), who started the restaurant on the site of their drive-in movie place.

This rustic eatery features charbroiled steaks, chicken-fried steaks, and barbecued sausage and beef.

The Big Al's New York strip steak is aged heavy beef and comes with green salad, french fries or baked potato, and homemade bread ($7.95). The jumbo chicken-fried steak comes with a green salad and french fries for $4.95. The cream gravy is as thick as gear grease. Edna told us, "The food disappears as quickly as we bring it out of the oven." That certainly is the case with their homemade coconut cream pie, which is made by Al's sister (95¢ a slice). "We can't keep up with the demand," Edna boasted.

The atmosphere is helped immensely by the fact that the walls are of old barn wood, which the owners had brought in from several barns they tore down on their ranch. Edna told us that when the wood was being put up, the carpenters had trouble cutting it with their saws.

The restaurant has many antiques on display, but not for sale. You *can* buy heavenly quilts made by local ladies ($275–325), meats, cheeses, breads, and even their homemade barbecue sauce.

US Hwy. 181
(512) 583-2113
Thursday–Tuesday 9:30 a.m.–9 p.m.

Kerrville

HILL COUNTRY CAFE

*T*he waitresses at the Hill Country Cafe have a habit of photographing their customers and hanging the pictures on the cafe walls, so dress for posterity if you decide to stop in. And speaking of dress, don't be surprised if the waitresses are dressed alike. They do that for special occasions; last Christmas they all showed up as elves.

Chris Manning has owned this well-known cafe for only a year, but in that short time he has established a reputation for good, honest food. They make biscuits from scratch and process their own potatoes for french fries, mashed potatoes, and hash browns. Lunch specials include liver and onions, chicken-fried steak, fried catfish, roast beef, and both fried and baked chicken. You also get your choice of two vegetables, a salad or coleslaw, iced tea or coffee, and a piece of cake or pie, all for just $3.50.

The cafe is popular with the movers and shakers around Kerrville; the mayor and a table of his friends have coffee there almost every day.

806 Main
(512) 896-5290
Monday–Friday 5:30 a.m.–2 p.m.
Saturday 5:30 a.m.–11 a.m.
(breakfast only)

New Braunfels

KRAUSE'S CAFE

*T*he late Gene Krause started this cafe back in 1938 as a place that served chili, stew, and hamburgers. Today the menu is as diverse as a department store—there's everything from steaks to ham sandwiches to sauerkraut. Don't miss their famous pies—twenty to choose from. Other local favorites are Krause's cornbread and biscuits; they're made from scratch. Now the cafe is run by Gene's son and daughter-in-law, Kermit and Mildred.

This is a famous landmark cafe, so it certainly would be worth your time to grab a bite to eat. In New York, eat at "21"; in New Braunfels, Krause's.

148 S. Castell
(512) 625-7581
Monday–Saturday 6:30 a.m.–8:30 p.m.

Pontotoc

PONTOTOC INN

*D*on't blink or you'll miss this. The Pontotoc Inn is a small old brown metal building with tin siding that serves as a post office and cafe to the folks around these parts. The cafe and post office (all in the same building) are both run by Betty Waldron. She's the postmaster.

The restaurant serves fried catfish, steaks, and quail, as well as Mexican food, hamburgers, and a wide selection of sandwiches. Betty's homemade desserts include cream pies, cobblers, and even strawberry shortcake.

This is a popular place for people traveling between Brady and Llano. With its seating capacity of thirty-two, things can get really crowded. But you'll find your fellow diners to be friendly and helpful in case you feel a touch off the beaten track and lost.

For your information, Pontotoc is the Mississippi hometown of one of this tiny town's settlers.

Texas Hwy. 71
(915) 251-6667
Monday noon—2 p.m.
Wednesday—Friday 8:30 a.m.—8:30 p.m.

Temple

BLUE BONNET CAFE

*K*nown statewide for its chicken-fried steak, the Blue Bonnet Cafe has been touted and revered nearly all of its thirty-six years in business. This is the type of cafe that exudes a friendly, established small-town atmosphere. Efficient waitresses mind the orders of senior citizens, couples with small children, and customers who have visited patients in the well-known Santa Fe Hospital across the street. The owners, Laverne Pitts and George and Susan Luck, seem to know each customer and have a friendly smile or a word readily available.

The menu has many southern favorites, including fried chicken, catfish, and pork chops. You can also choose homemade Irish stew or Mexican dishes. A daily special of a meat and three vegetables arrives with a salad, hot rolls, homemade cornbread, a drink, and a dessert.

Paintings of fields of bluebonnets adorn the walls, and in the spring, fresh bluebonnets are placed on each table—a gift from one of the regulars. On your way out, you can purchase a sweet or maybe a Lovera cigar from the glass case, which also holds mementos.

The Blue Bonnet Cafe is a Texas tradition.

705 S. 25th
(817) 773-6654
Friday—Wednesday 6 a.m.—9 p.m.

Wimberley

CYPRESS CREEK CAFE

*T*his cafe serves blue plate specials but tries to add a dash of flare that makes the food "country cuisine." A former cook from Ouisie's restaurant in Houston, Mary Margaret Westbrook is in the kitchen and helps prepare the menu, which ranges from chicken-fried steak, fried catfish, and chicken breasts to beef liver with a choice of vegetables (they say "veggies"), mashed potatoes, and black beans. A blue plate special will cost you $4.50. Or you can have the dinner favorite: barbecued shrimp or butterflied charbroiled shrimp, choice of vegetables, dinner salad, and baked potato or french fries, for $8.95.

In the morning have a breakfast taco. A ten-inch flour tortilla loaded with scrambled eggs, cheddar cheese, homemade salsa, and sausage is just $2.45. It takes two hands to eat.

The bakery upstairs has ex—Austin resident Joanna Johnson preparing delicious pies. The Katharine Hepburn pie, which is based on the star's actual brownie recipe, is heavenly at $1.75 a square.

Our advice is to eat your meal, go browse through this lovely lazy town, including its antique stores, then return for a slice of pie. You won't feel quite as sinful.

On the square
(512) 847-2515
Tuesday—Saturday 7 a.m.—9 p.m.
Sunday 7 a.m.—2 p.m.

Southeast

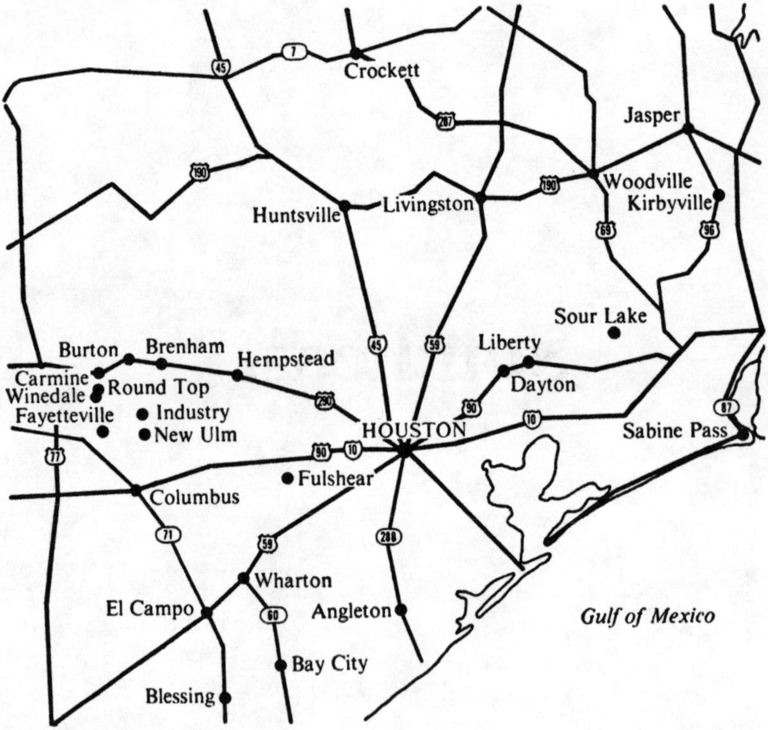
Crockett
Jasper
Woodville
Kirbyville
Huntsville
Livingston
Sour Lake
Burton
Brenham
Hempstead
Liberty
Carmine
Winedale
Round Top
Dayton
Fayetteville
Industry
New Ulm
HOUSTON
Sabine Pass
Fulshear
Columbus
Wharton
El Campo
Angleton
Gulf of Mexico
Bay City
Blessing

Angleton

ANGIE'S

The piped-in song "I've Been Working on the Railroad" is the only artifact missing from Angie's, which hugs the railroad tracks inside and out. The walls are decorated with lanterns, engines from electric trains, and railroad signs. Even the menu has a train with a stop sign on it. The children's menu is called Little Conductors. Regular customers include the self-named railroad gang: Norman "Captain" Kirk, "Fast" Fred Hall, Rick Freeman, and T. W. Oliver. It is a good idea to get there early; lunch is served from 11 to 2, and with such popular items as chicken and dumplings on the menu, standing room only is often the rule. Angie also serves such dishes as roast beef, baked pork chops, and fried chicken, garnished with an available fresh vegetable, all for $4.10, coffee or tea included.

Angie's pies and cobblers are so popular that she frequently sells them before they are taken out of the oven. Choices range from apple, pecan, and cherry to chocolate, coconut cream, and lemon cream.

We can recommend the chicken and dumplings, but the mounds of fried onion rings for 85¢ looked real inviting, too.

500 S. Velasco
(409) 849-3004
Monday—Saturday 6 a.m.—9 p.m.
Sundays 6 a.m.—2 p.m.

Bay City

TOWN SQUARE CAFE

A new cafe by most cafe standards, Town Square Cafe is aptly named due to its location on the square. It has only about two years to its track record, but Adella Holland says, "I treat people like they were in my home. Sometimes I raise cain. I treat customers like family." Her customers range from merchants, bankers, and county courthouse workers to travelers, school kids, and hospital visitors. She has a family-run business, with daughter Susan Busch as a waitress and her two sons Eugene and Eddie Martin helping where needed. Frances is her head cook, but Adella's mother-in-law pitches in, too.

Breakfast is served all day. After two o'clock, most customers come in for fresh-brewed tea or coffee and maybe a dice game.

Adella's Town Square Cafe offers a wide variety of food on a menu that changes daily. But you are always guaranteed a meat and two fresh vegetables (seasonally grown in Grandpa's garden), cornbread or rolls, desserts, and coffee or tea for $5.20, tax included. All their soups are homemade, too: vegetable beef, potato, and chicken noodle. Home-cooked chili, too. We had chicken and dumplings. They were reminiscent of someone's family recipe that we remembered from a long time ago. We hope Adella is serving them when you're there.

We noted several times how clean, sunny, tidy, and well-run this cafe was. Adella says, "We recognize all credit cards, but accept only cash."

2139 Avenue G
(409) 245-1269
Monday—Saturday 6:30 a.m.—4 p.m.

Blessing

HOTEL BLESSING COFFEE SHOP

*I*n 1907, when the railroad arrived at last, Jonathan Edward Pierce wanted to name his town "Thank God," but the local landowners kept saying what a "blessing" the railroad's arrival was; thus, the name "Blessing" stuck. (This is one of four similar stories we have heard on how the name came about.)

Indeed, a blessing it is today to have this well-preserved historical hotel and coffee shop emulating life at the turn of the century. The building has a wraparound porch that catches the breeze. Each room in the hotel has screened windows and is furnished with iron beds, handmade quilts, pine dressers, and perhaps a bentwood rocker. The nightly rate for a single without bath is $15, and a double without bath goes for $20. Rooms with a bath rent for $20 and $25. There are weekly rates, too.

But it's the coffee shop where all the real action is. Big breakfasts of eggs, pancakes, and meat are available for under $3. Or, if you really time it right, you can eat lunch here. The buffet choices include chicken-fried steak and roast beef. On Wednesday you can have meat loaf, on Thursday chicken, on Friday catfish, and on Saturday chicken-fried steak. On Sunday, well, owner Helen Feldhousen says, "It's just like Christmas." She serves turkey, ham, or roast beef, with eight vegetables to choose from (seasonally fresh). The daily specials are $4.50, and the Sunday buffet is $4.95.

You serve yourself from the buffet line at old gas stoves with the food in pots and pans on top. You dine family-style and eat with what seems like all of the Blessing's population of 300: ranchers, travelers, power plant workers, you name it. If you have any room left, try the homemade desserts.

10th and Ave. B
(512) 588-6623
Open seven days, 6 a.m.–2 p.m.

Brenham

DAVID'S CORNER CAFE

*T*his cafe was named after owner Mary Belle Nowicki's son, who works in the family's meat market next door. Needless to say, the market supplies the staples for the daily menu of hot roast beef and chicken-fried steak and for the rotating specials of ham, barbecued sausage, pork, chicken, and meat loaf. When possible, Mrs. Nowicki buys her vegetables, including black-eyed peas, cabbage, and lima beans, from local sources. The sauerkraut, corn, and green peas are canned and the mashed potatoes instant, but they taste just fine, which goes to show that a little seasoning and tender loving care make a big difference. For lunch you can choose one meat, three vegetables, a dessert, and a drink for just $3.50.

The highlight of David's Corner, though, is the dominoes game. Players drift in every day after two o'clock (that's the only time Mrs. Nowicki will allow them to play) for another round in a game that has been going on for the last thirty years.

109 Commerce
(409) 836-0810
Monday–Saturday 7 a.m.–9 p.m.
Sunday noon–11 or 12 p.m.

SCHOENEMANN'S RESTAURANT

*B*renham is so close to Houston that it is in jeopardy of losing its integrity as a small Texas town. It has become one of the most chic weekend places in the country for city dwellers. Imagine the hundred-mile migration that begins every Friday afternoon as many of Houston's power hitters shed their Brooks Brothers suits for blue jeans and denim shirts. We've seen country places in Brenham with indoor swimming pools, tennis courts, helipads, jet landing strips, four-bedroom guest houses, and all manner of horse stables and arenas. The point is that these well-heeled Houstonians gobble up everything "country" with the enthusiasm of a child in a candy store. One such country attraction is Schoenemann's.

Schoenemann's Cafe is in downtown Brenham, so at lunch one gets an interesting mix of city officials, professionals, shop owners, nearby farmers, students, and, of course, Houstonians.

For our money, Burford and Ruth Schoenemann make the best yeast rolls anywhere. Like their bread, the rolls are homemade and baked fresh daily. For less than $5, you can choose between chicken-fried steak or pork roast, and along with your meat and homemade bread and rolls and salad and dessert and coffee or tea come mountains of hot vegetables: green beans, carrots, mashed potatoes, cream corn.

Other items on the luncheon menu are steaks, pork chops, fried chicken, and such, but why bother? Your best bet is to eat what Burford and Ruth and cook Thelma Charles have made specially for the day.

210 E. Alamo
(409) 836-9441
Monday–Saturday 5 a.m.–2 p.m.

Burton

BURTON'S CAFE

*T*here are two reasons to visit Burton's Cafe, maybe three. The first is to try the cafe-made pie for only 70¢ a slice (chocolate, coconut cream, buttermilk, apple, and peach, among others). The second reason is to listen to the chatter on the cafe's blaring police and fire radio receiver. The third is to see the chair that actor Larry Hagman autographed while in the neighborhood to check on his oil investments. He arrived in a helicopter and gave owner Rosalie Powell his souvenir $100 bill. (It says, "This note isn't worth the paper it's printed on.") The bill is now—of course—proudly displayed in the cafe.

Spur 125
(Behind the old post office)
(409) 289-3849
Monday—Saturday 7 a.m.—9 p.m.

Carmine

VILLAGE CAFE

What a pleasant surprise. Dolly Armatys, owner of the Village Cafe for the past three years, is also a friend of our favorite aunt and uncle, Elizabeth and Carroll Kennard of Anderson, Texas. Texas isn't so big after all.

Dolly's customers say "she serves the best hamburgers in the state of Texas." We know the secret. Dolly's meat is 100 percent pure fresh ground beef. This means it has no additives. It is the way meat really is before it gets processed for general consumption. For $2.15 you can experience this freshness on a bun. Dolly also serves fresh sirloin ($7.50), T-bone steak ($6.50), chicken-fried steak ($5.40), and hamburger steak ($5.10). French fries and salad are included with all entrées. There are also homemade pies: chocolate, apple, and coconut cream, at 75¢ a slice. Lemon chiffon and chocolate cake are also 75¢ a slice. You'll like their homemade breads, too. "We are just serving plain country cooking—good quality food," Dolly says.

214 Main
(409) 278-3257
Monday–Thursday 7 a.m.–9:30 p.m.
Friday–Saturday 7 a.m.–10:00 p.m.
Sunday 11 a.m.

Columbus

CITY CAFE

*F*or the last twenty-eight years Grandma Hertha David (pronouned Dah-vid) has fired up the ovens at the City Cafe at about six every morning. When we arrived at ten we were almost bowled over by several people apparently on their way to a mid-morning feast at a local business, staggering under boxes of fresh kolaches. Besides these ham- or fruit-filled Czech pastries, Grandma Hertha makes bread, cinnamon buns, dinner rolls, and pies. She bakes only once a day, so when something runs out, that's it.

But the City Cafe isn't just a bakery. It's a family cafe operation as well. Aunt Nancy and Aunt Margie grow fresh vegetables in the summer, while their daughter and son-in-law provide all the cafe's meats. Granddaughter JoAnn waits on your table with baby Zachary in tow. Son Billy, a passionate fisherman, has two largemouth bass hung judiciously on the wall, as if there will be more to come.

The chicken-fried steaks we had for lunch were so huge they hung over the plates. The gravy was slightly lumpy, but the meat had been hand-breaded. Our meal, one meat and a choice of three vegetables, was less than $3.

The City Cafe once tried to switch to frozen french fries, but the regulars complained so much that the Davids reconsidered. Every Wednesday the lunch special is Mexican food, all homemade.

500 block of Walnut
(409) 732-8009
Monday—Saturday 6 a.m.—5 p.m.
Sunday 6 a.m.—1 p.m.

Crockett

ROYAL RESTAURANT

*T*he Royal Restaurant has seventy years of continuous service under its apron. It is indeed one of the oldest cafes we visited. Situated on the town square with a jumbo neon sign beckoning you in, it's not hard to find.

When word got around that previous owner Nathan Shroyer was retiring, Judy Whitley, then the owner of Judy's Drive-In, saw a way of making her dreams come true. She now owns the Royal, and her daughter Glenda McDonald is the manager.

The buffet spread at lunch is a big attraction, with different choices available daily. We visited on a Wednesday and had Sally Rhodes's "famous in Crockett parts" chicken and dumplings—big chunks of chicken with homemade dumplings floating in a home-style chicken broth. This was served along with black-eyed peas, macaroni and cheese, cornbread muffins, pie or pudding, and a salad, all for $4.75.

We learned that on Mondays they serve chicken-fried steak that chef J. D. Barnett proudly oversees. He cuts and trims each portion of the meat himself. When you order one, it may take a little longer than some places because J. D. "fixes each one as the order comes up." It is dredged in a seasoned flour mixture, egg, and milk, and then deep-fried. It's worth the wait. Steaks are a big item here at night, with just about all types served. But what isn't commonplace is that J. D. also cuts each T-bone, rib eye, filet, and sirloin himself from fresh sides of beef. The 10 to 6 shift is a busy one, too. Hunters, truck drivers, locals who work late shifts, and "all kinds," Glenda says, keep them going.

You're in Davy Crockett country, in case you didn't know. He camped nearby on his way to the Alamo. Two marvelous tile murals that depict the life of this Texas hero are on the dining room walls of the Royal. Of special interest is the nineteen-point deer head on the wall. Count 'em yourself.

On the square
(409) 544-3863
Open seven days, 24 hours

Dayton

GRANDMA'S KITCHEN

We pulled into Dayton on a Tuesday needing fuel—for our car and our bodies. The gas station attendant directed us to Grandma's, and off we went. Grandma's is in a home that dates somewhere after Victorian, but before the 1950s. It has housed many small businesses. Easily seen from the road, it has a coat of bright blue paint, which makes it look all the crisper. The inside doesn't resemble the outside. It's decorated with shag carpet, paneled walls, and very clean tables. Pat Meadows is busy cooking and taking orders right along with her mother, Irene Barnes.

They sell a lot of baked potatoes ($1.10) with a wide selection of stuffings (60¢), in case you don't like 'em just buttered. Pat and Irene also offer hamburgers ($1.70) and bowls of homemade chili ($1.20) and vegetable soup ($1.20). They post daily specials that might be chicken and dumplings, chicken-fried steak, or beef tips with rice and mashed potatoes, cream gravy, a vegetable, and rolls, all for $3.15. Fresh-brewed tea and soft drinks are also available.

For dessert, Pat says her mom makes "every kind" of pie. We had chocolately chocolate. If you arrive for breakfast, they serve up a big one—two eggs, choice of patty sausage, sliced ham, or bacon, house hash browns or grits, homemade biscuits, and gravy for $2.75.

Don't be shy; go to the window, place your order, get a number, sit back, and wait for home cooking like Grandma did.

704 FM Rd. 1960
(409) 258-9153
Monday—Friday 8 a.m.—4 p.m.
Saturday 8:30 a.m.—2:30 p.m.

El Campo

EL CAMPO LIVESTOCK CAFE

With hours like these, it's best to get here early. This is where Helen Feldhousen hangs her pots and pans when her Blessing Hotel Coffee shop is closed. Her menu is chicken-fried steak, vegetables, french fries, and gravy with a drink and dessert for $4.

Plan all trips to El Campo on Tuesday.

Texas Hwy. 71
(409) 543-2703
Tuesdays only, 11:30 a.m. till the pots are empty

RODDY'S DONUT SHOP AND CAFE

*T*he word "cafe" on the sign is faded, but the painted slogan above the well-worn screen doors—"Where old and new friends meet"—is persuasive. The whitewashed wooden-sided cafe sits across El Campo's railroad tracks from the El Campo Rice Milling Company. The small unobtrusive building is kept cool by a bountiful pecan tree that gives shade on a warm Texas day.

Ethel Roddy and her sons Glenn and Dennis are the proprietors of this counter and five-table eatery. Mr. Roddy passed away in 1979, and the cafe menu has changed as a result. There are no more grits and eggs, but they do offer such fare as early morning pastries and coffee. This has been a gathering spot for El Campo residents, businessmen, and travelers for more than sixteen years. Old habits die hard.

The morning menu is simple, but everything is homemade by Ethel and Dennis: donuts 20¢, cinnamon rolls 30¢, pig-n-blankets (jalapeño and cheese with sausage), fresh fruit-filled kolaches, and apricot fried pies. With the fresh-brewed coffee at 25¢, you can dine scrumptiously for less than $1.

"If we don't please you tell us, not others" is on a sign above the checkout counter. Mrs. Roddy says they get few complaints—so few, in fact, that her other son Royce and his wife Betty have opened a spinoff in Clute, Texas, called the Kolache Shop. They are using Ethel's time-tested recipes. Clute diners are in luck.

201 S. Washington
(409) 543-1493
Tuesday—Saturday
7 a.m.—midnight

Fayetteville

MICHALSKY'S CAFE

*S*ophie Michalsky has been decorating this place for more than twenty-one years now. The result is unparalleled cafe kitsch. Besides the Coke machine and jukebox, she has velvet paintings from Mexico and a scale that dispenses fortunes. Those items mingle with sombreros dangling from deer antlers, Shiner beer calendars picturing dogs playing poker, gimme caps, plastic birds on perches hanging from the ceiling, old Christmas cards, wrought-iron ships, and even an award that Sophie's husband Jerry received in 1982 from the American Institute of Architects for some fancy carpentry that he did.

But no matter how cluttered and chaotic the decor, the menu is straightforward and simple. Sophie calls it "Take what I got," and regular customers phone ahead to find out if a favorite dish is on the stove. The vegetables are fresh whenever possible, and she makes pies when she can. Jerry likes dewberry pie so much that he picks the berries himself. Sounds like a great bet during dewberry season in April.

One caution: from the outside, the place looks dreary. There is only one window and nothing else to invite you in, but take our word for it—the decorations alone are worth the experience.

**On the square
(409) 378-9255
Open seven days, 7 a.m.–2 p.m.
and 5 p.m.–9 p.m.**

ORSAK'S CAFE

*O*n the one and only square in Fayetteville, just a biscuit's throw from Michalsky's Cafe, is Ike and Edith Orsak's place. We had a solid country breakfast here of smoked ham, eggs, and hash browns; and Ike, a taciturn type who takes pride in the food he serves, made us some real hot chocolate. Lunch specials include fried chicken, fried fish, barbecue, and anything else Ike and Edith feel like fixing. One of the best reasons to go to Orsak's, though, is to read the multitudinous signs on the wall. Apparently what Ike lacks in talkativeness, he makes up for with signs, especially funny ones to improve your disposition and make your coffee last a little longer. The Orsak community bulletin board is worth a look-see, too.

**On the square
(409) 378-2719
Tuesday–Sunday 7 a.m.–6 p.m.
Monday 7 a.m.–2 p.m.**

Fulshear

DOZIER'S GROCERY MARKET

When Houstonians want a quick fix of country atmosphere and food, they head for Fulshear, to a place called Dozier's Market. Fulshear is about an hour's drive from Houston, depending on what part of the day you leave. (Hint: leave early or not at all.)

Dozier's Market has been in operation for more than twenty years. The original owner, Ed Dozier, sold the market and restaurant to the Evans family in October 1985, but the new owners' attitude about the operation is pretty clear-cut: "If it ain't broke, don't fix it." That's a good guarantee that the fixin's will remain the same as they were during the Dozier regime.

Dozier's is a meat market, grocery store, and—in the back—a "Chow Room," all under one roof. Outside you'll find picnic tables and, on the side, a sort of beer-garden atmosphere where you can dine on pleasant summer days. The meat is pecan smoked, and you can buy brisket, sausage, ribs, and, on the weekends, chicken. A plate of barbecue with two meats will cost you $4.50, and a barbecue sandwich is $2.25. The plate dinners come with pinto beans, coleslaw, or potato salad.

The meat market sells steaks, ground beef, smoked hams, and

turkeys. The Chow Room only holds six tables—about thirty-six people—so call ahead for a reading on the crowd or come early. The food is good and the atmosphere perfect.

300 Main
(713) 346-1411
Tuesday–Thursday 8 a.m.–6:30 p.m.
Friday and Saturday 8 a.m.–7 p.m.
Sunday 10 a.m.–7 p.m.

Hempstead

HEMPSTEAD INN

*T*o appreciate the Hempstead Inn, you have to have a little background on Hempstead. Even though the town is close to Houston, just forty-eight miles away, the silk stocking crowd has always bypassed it. Hempstead is not a particularly pretty place. It's a workingman's kind of town. The main street is really a four-lane highway with a continuous stream of trucks and passenger cars screaming by. So it struck us as strange that someone was actually trying, in this rough-and-tumble territory, to run an inn with class and dignity. But there it is, right there by the side of the highway: the Hempstead Inn.

The Hempstead Inn is a large two-story frame structure, painted a gray-blue. It has a large covered front porch, and there is ample parking on the side. The building would be more impressive if it were surrounded by lots of green lawn, but since it was once a railroad hotel, there is nary a blade.

Inside we felt a little uncomfortable, but that was only because we weren't sure what we were supposed to do. Over that awkward little moment, however, we found ourselves sitting family-style at long tables with eager waitresses handing us bowls of mashed potatoes and other delectables. The day we were there, we had an endless supply of fried chicken and fish plus a variety of fresh vegetables. Hempstead, you have to remember, has developed a reputation for growing vegetables. It has been made famous by a roadside market and farm operation not far from the Hempstead Inn, called DiLorio Farm and Roadside Market. When you drive by DiLorio's you'll recognize it because it looks like a Safeway store that has had a whole side wall opened up. There will probably be about fifty cars parked in front; it's a very popular market.

The Hempstead Inn is owned by Ghazi and Maryanne Issa; while they no longer accept overnight guests, the inn serves a nice meal that you can enjoy before hitting the home stretch to Houston. Lunch buffet will cost you $6, and dinner served family-style is $8. Everything is fresh, including Maryanne's terrific cobblers.

435 10th (US Hwy. 290)
(409) 826-6379
Tuesday–Friday 11 a.m.–2 p.m.
Saturday and Sunday 11 a.m.–10 p.m.

Huntsville

CAFE TEXAN

*I*f you ever have to go to Huntsville and need a good place to eat, the Cafe Texan is the place. Established in 1936, it has been managed continuously by Vernon Todd. In fact, in a strange web of corporate oddity, Vernon was at one time its owner as well. It's a long story, but Vernon will be happy to tell you. The Cafe Texan is owned by Doug (Bo) Bertling now. Bo's a pleasant man who obviously had the good sense to keep Vernon around.

This downtown cafe specializes in chicken-fried and pepper steaks. You can always count on breakfast to be good, too. Two eggs, grits, and hot rolls with ham, bacon, or sausage will cost you about $2, and it's available all day. Of course, the cafe has a wide variety of short-order items available from the menu, as well.

Huntsville is home of the Texas Department of Corrections. The town's population is nearly twenty-five thousand; six thousand of those people work for the prison, and another seven thousand are in the prison. Dan Rather, Dana Andrews, and Steve Forrest are among the celebrities who have eaten at the Cafe Texan.

Of special interest to us were their homemade pies. The chocolate pie made with real chocolate is wonderful.

1120 Sam Houston
(409) 295-2381
Open seven days, 6 a.m.—9 p.m.

Industry

PINKY'S CAFE

*Y*ou have to really want to go to Pinky's to find it, because it certainly isn't on the way to anywhere big. But if you take the trouble, you're in for a treat. Pinky's is owned by Norma and Lloyd Wubbenhorst, who along with their son Roger and his wife, Patsy, have been running the cafe for more than six years.

Pinky's serves a generous hand-breaded chicken-fried steak, as well as great cream gravy made by Norma. Roger, a refugee from a 9 to 5 job in Houston, fixes memorable pinto beans, using a recipe he won't divulge. The food is made from fresh ingredients as much as possible. During our visit Roger was deep in negotiations with a local woman for fresh farm eggs. In the end he bought three dozen.

During the Austin Chalk boom, Pinky's was a bit more active, but it still enjoys the support of the local Lions Club. Note the 1950s gasoline pump (which no longer works) and the red, yellow, and pink roses in front. On the inside, don't miss the nickel Coke machine.

US Hwy. 159 (1.2 mi. southwest)
No phone
Tuesday–Friday 4 p.m.–10 p.m.
Saturday 9 a.m.–10 p.m.

Jasper

TEXAS CHARLIE'S

*T*exas Charlie's proclaims to be world famous, and if it is, it's a result of the cafe's varied menu. There's barbecue, Mexican food, T-bones, and, every Tuesday, a chicken-fried steak plate for $3.50. You eat family-style on long wooden tables with benches. Sip your drink from Ball jars that are used as glasses. Texas Charlie's also offers homemade cream pies, jellies, and gimme caps for sale.

"Please don't let me die while I'm on a diet" is a poster decorating the wall that says it all.

US Hwy. 96
(409) 384-4451
Monday—Friday 5:30 a.m.—9 p.m.
Saturday 5:30 a.m.—9:30 p.m.

Kirbyville

LITTLE HOUSE RESTAURANT

*J*ackie McKenzie and her sister, Martha Lackey, have been serving home-cooked meals for more than four years. Their efforts have not gone unappreciated. They have a large local following and a new dining room with a seating capacity of seventy-five to show for it.

The daily lunch special is a choice of one meat from pickin's of three and three vegetables from seven. The vegetables are fresh when available or have a just-picked taste by virtue of the hand that cooks 'em. You get homemade yeast rolls, cornbread, your drink, and dessert, all for $3.75 (tax included). The desserts can be anything from peach or apple cobbler to bread pudding, banana pudding, or cake.

If there's just too much to take in from the steam table, try their homemade chili or Mexican food.

If you happen to be there for breakfast, you'll find, besides the usual eggs, hash browns, and grits, some homemade biscuits to soak up cream gravy. There's a big welcome sign hanging outside. They don't need it.

417 N. Margarete
(409) 423-5312
Monday—Friday 7 a.m.—8 p.m.
Saturday 7 a.m.—4 p.m.

Liberty

LAYL'S SANDWICH SHOP

*L*ayl's Sandwich Shop is a perfect example of the treasures that have gotten bypassed by the Interstate Highway system. Layl's is situated on US Hwy. 90 in Liberty, halfway between Houston and Beaumont. Years ago, this highway was the main road between Florida and California. And back then, in the 1940s and '50s, when people actually drove from one coast to the other, Layl's was a booming business.

But while business isn't booming as it once did, there's still a lot to like about this cafe. For one thing, it's an exquisite example of an Art Deco interior. Even if they didn't serve food there, it would be worth a visit. On the inside, the walls are done in black and white tiles. Windows are an interesting octagonal shape, and the interior sparkles with chrome and glass. In fact, Layl's lunch counter is exactly what a lunch counter should look like; it should be preserved for its historical importance.

Layl's is owned by Paul Blansett, a man who is as interesting as his cafe. If he takes a liking to you, he might just pull out a recipe as a gift or even a jar of pickled okra, cucumbers, or peppers.

Lunch specials change daily here, but you can always depend on the chicken-fried steak and the barbecued chicken. The luncheon special with two vegetables, dessert, and coffee or iced tea will cost you around $4.

Of interest to us was the fact that one Clara Gunter actually worked at this cafe for fifty-one years. In fact, Clara was one of the first female carhops in Texas. She retired only a couple of years ago. (Layl's offered curb service back in its heyday.)

Pull up a chair and enjoy a meal in a place where Will Rogers, Wiley Post, Glen McCarthy, Danny Thomas, and John Mecom, Sr., have all eaten.

2118 Commerce
(409) 336-3531
Open seven days, 5 a.m.–9 p.m.

CHICKEN SHACK

Just down the road a couple of blocks from Layl's Sandwich Shop is the Chicken Shack. As the name implies, this small restaurant sells fried chicken—but only to go. Owner James Evans cooks and sells just this one item, but he does it very well. His fried chicken is some of the best we've ever tasted. He also serves a unique fried honey roll, which is a work of art. It comes with your chicken, and James even gives you real honey, which you either spread on your chicken or dip your roll into.

As you will be able to tell from the exterior, this place used to be a gas station. In busier times it was also a bus station and housed a Western Union operator. The Chicken Shack isn't a cafe, but it's one of those tiny treasures that's worth the stop.

2024 Commerce
No phone
Monday–Friday 10 a.m.–3 p.m.

Livingston

SLAYDEN'S CAFE

"*T*his is the towners' place," my husband's son Jonas said to me when we pulled up. And it's a very popular place, too, if the crowd eating there was any indication. Joan and Don Slayden share the proprietorship, but Joan oversees the cafe on a day-to-day basis. Don flies a helicopter for Mobil Oil out of Morgan City, Louisiana, and gets one week on and one week off. During his time off he helps out.

Slayden's boast is that they specialize in good food and that they prepare it all from scratch on the premises daily. It's a lot to live up to, but from all reports at our table, they're doing it. The daily special is a meat and two vegetables for $3.95. Meat selections are served with Louisiana red beans and rice. We sampled this side dish and found it just right. Slayden's also offers chicken pot pie, pork chops, and catfish on Fridays. Vegetables are fresh when in season. Your meal will also come with home-made biscuits, Texas toast, and cornbread—all to be chased down by either fresh-brewed iced tea at 55¢ or 100 percent Columbian coffee at 35¢. Joan says, "It's fresh or someone will be fired."

If this doesn't tempt your palate, you can also choose from hamburgers and barbecue of all varieties. The barbecue is cooked in a pit out back. Joan told us, "We don't slice it until we need to. It keeps moist that way." The hamburger patties are made daily from fresh-ground meat. They are high priced at $2.25, but Joan says, "They're better quality." Hamburger fixin's include chopped Texas onions and a buttered grilled bun, as well as the usual lettuce, pickle, and tomato. We saw plates piled high with orders of home-cooked french fries that looked like natural partners to a meal.

Joan told us she had been a legal secretary. She and her husband use the same recipes from the twenty-three-year-old Slayden's barbecue in Bastrop, Louisiana, without varying even a quarter-teaspoon.

Menna Smith has the responsibility of duplicating Don's mother's (Helen Slayden's) pie recipes. We don't think we've ever had better. Every day they have one fruit pie and one cream pie. Our choice was apple, and it was served with Blue Bell vanilla ice cream for $1.05. We had our eyes on the coconut cream, too. Whole pies are available for $6.75, and cobblers are $12.75. Fresh strawberry pies are available in March, April, and May.

There's a sign on Slayden's Cafe that says, "Thin may be in, but fat's where it's at!" That's something to consider.

705 N. Washington
(409) 327-2750
Monday–Saturday 6 a.m.–8 p.m.

New Ulm

PARLOUR RESTAURANT

We can't really say that the Parlour Restaurant is a cafe, but we can tell you that it's worth a visit. First, it is in New Ulm, which is barely a town—not because it doesn't have residents, because it does. The town is just so oddly laid out. One block will be filled with buildings, and the next one will have only a few. You get the impression that a lot used to happen here, but it doesn't seem to be happening now.

In the middle of this helter-skelter collection of buildings is the Parlour Restaurant, housed in a structure that once contained a funeral home. Another part of the building's history is evidenced by the holes that were drilled in the floor after the hurricane of 1900 to drain water out.

The Parlour is owned by New Ulm natives Edna and Alton Haverlah. Once himself a prisoner of war, Alton boasts that he will give any American former POW free beer at the Parlour.

On the menu side, Alton—who has owned the restaurant since 1975—serves cafe-like food, including a pretty good chicken-fried steak, fresh vegetables from the Houston Farmers Market, and fresh-frozen seafood and homemade bread.

On the weekends there's live music, big crowds, and a lot of confusion. Definitely make reservations. In the summer you'll want to sample one of eight draft beers available, as well as the beer garden outside. If you suspect the area was settled by Germans, you're right.

1 Front
(409) 992-3499
Tuesday—Sunday 11 a.m.—10 p.m.

Round Top

ROUND TOP CAFE

*T*his is a lifestyle that causes a trapped Houstonian to weep. Owner Dick Peck is a Pan Am pilot who flies out of Houston to New York four or five times a month. The rest of the time he and his wife Sherry reside in the picturesque town of Round Top and run the cafe. The cook has been in residence for fifteen years and serves an unbeatable chicken-fried steak. The large one is eight ounces (a small one is available, too) and is hand-breaded, fried, and smothered with cooked onions (gravy if you request). It's served with french fries and salad for $6.50. On weekends they have barbecued pork loin, beef, sausage, and chicken. A $3.95 plate comes with sauerkraut, beans, cold German potato salad, and home-style buttered noodles.

Look over the Lone Star player piano. If you find a music roll you want to play, feel free to do so, or ask the waitress. If you do play the piano, don't be shy. Acclaimed pianist James Dick has also tinkled these ivories.

On the square
(409) 249-3611
Tuesday—11 a.m.—3 p.m.
Wednesday 11 a.m.—9 p.m.
Thursday 11 a.m.—8 p.m.
Friday, Saturday—8 a.m.—9 p.m.
Sunday—8 a.m.—5 p.m.

Sabine Pass

DESLATT'S

*T*he first thing you have to understand about Deslatt's is that it's across the street from a much larger and more famous restaurant—Sartin's. But whether you eat at Sartin's or Deslatt's, you can't go wrong. Each is a different but equally satisfying experience, and, in fact, the owners are related. They're cousins.

Carole Deslatt has owned this cafe for ten years, and it serves breakfast, lunch, and dinner to a loyal group of local folks. The building itself is close to a hundred years old, but additions and remodeling will make it hard for you to notice that. The interior is presently decorated with seafood nets and crabs.

The dinner we had and the one we strongly recommend is the barbecued crab and fried shrimp platter for $8.95. The meal comes with seafood gumbo, home french fries or stuffed potato, and a trip to a better-than-average salad bar.

The cafe is a pleasant, easy-paced place with a good country and western jukebox. Their fresh seafood is brought in daily by members of the family who own their own fishing boats—a guarantee of freshness.

On the square
(409) 971-9200
Monday–Saturday 6 a.m.–10 p.m.
Sunday 11 a.m.–7 p.m.

SARTIN'S

*E*ver wonder what four hundred people sound like cracking crab shells? Wonder no more. Welcome to Sartin's. From its humble beginnings as a few picnic tables, Sartin's has grown to somewhat of an East Texas tradition in just a little more than fifteen years.

While conventional dining is certainly allowed, most diners opt for the "platter service," which means you are served an array of fresh seafood, one platter after another, until you more or less surrender. Our courses included cold boiled crab claws, fried fish, barbecued blue crabs, stuffed crab, fried frog legs, fried shrimp, french fries, and hushpuppies. For $11.95, it's an all-you-can-eat extravaganza of the first order. In case that's not enough, for another $2 you can get raw or fried oysters, as well.

It's a casual atmosphere, with the tables covered in red oilcloth. Garbage cans are set beside each table so you can dispose of your shells after each course; rolls of paper towels are provided to wipe your hands with. Get the picture? Never dress up when you go to Sartin's.

The restaurant is decorated with old advertising signs, neon beer signs, deer heads, mounted crabs (which have been brought in over the years by generous customers), and other seaside memorabilia.

Luncheon specials vary but usually include homemade seafood gumbo or shrimp creole, salad, and two vegetables for $4.95, as well as pork chops with salad and two vegetables for $3.95.

The restaurant is owned and operated by Charles and Jerri Sartin, with the help of their children, Kelli and Douglas. Other members of the Sartin family provide the fresh seafood from their own fishing boats, so chances are good that what you are eating was caught the same morning in the Gulf.

Reservations are suggested on the weekends.

Texas Hwy. 87 at Tremont
(409) 971-2158
Open seven days, 11 a.m.—10 p.m.

Sour Lake

H-H COUNTRY KITCHEN CAFE

*J*oyce Hatcher's husband "always thought she was a good cook," so when the chance came to open a cafe on the spur of the moment, she did. Her cafe sign boasts "home cooking." Indeed it is. Every day, Joyce has chicken-fried steak, steak and gravy, and beef tips, plus two other specialties, along with nine vegetables (fresh or frozen and never canned) from which to choose. There's also homemade cornbread and rolls, and you can choose from three different salads. You have the hard choice of one meat and three vegetables for $3.85. Homemade apple pie goes for 80¢ a slice.

Many travelers have entered Joyce's establishment—people from as far away as Canada, Alaska, and Wisconsin. Her favorite story is about the people from England who had never had cornbread before. She said, "They didn't know what it was. They even took pictures."

The artesian well that lured hundreds for therapeutic reasons and had a real sour smell is gone now, but travelers still make their way to Sour Lake. And often to the H-H Country Kitchen Cafe.

244 E. Texas Hwy. 105
(409) 287-2430
Monday–Friday 7 a.m.–3:30 p.m.

Wharton

PEPPER'S

*A*n hour from Houston, nestled comfortably on the town square in a city that has been proclaimed a bird sanctuary, is "maybe the largest cafe in Texas." The 5,500-square-foot Pepper's is located in the space where the Duke & Ayers dime store was for forty-three years. In case you get lost on the square, look for a green neon cactus sign in the window.

The tin ceiling and original wood floors lend authenticity to Pepper's, which occupies just one of the many buildings on this square that date from the early 1900s. Owner Peggy Morton has decorated Pepper's with antiques ranging from rare splatterware jugs to muskets. If you want, you can have your picture taken with the statue of an old Indian couple, which Peggy relocates occasionally to keep customers on their toes. Chainsaw carvings by Pappy Joe of Arkansas and other less-well-known artists of the same craft adorn the walls, and vintage tin signs and a wooden carved schooner are also of interest.

Pepper's also features a Wharton Art League artist of the month. Peggy sells antiques on consignment and almost always offers locally produced honey and hand-carved products by a local boy who is retarded. Regulars sit or stand around playing chess, checkers, pinball, and pool.

After your senses try to take in this (and much more), you find your way to a handmade pine picnic table. If, like us, you stumbled by the tin buckets that hold the menus, it is not too late to retrieve one. Since Pepper's is what Peggy calls "a Texas type of place," its menu offers a wide array of home-cooked meals, all self-service. The hot lunch special can include a choice of hamburger steak, hot turkey sandwich, hot roast beef, or chicken-fried steak, served with a potato, vegetables (seasonally fresh), a trip to the salad bar, and Texas toast, all for $4.50. Your drink is extra, and the tea is served in twenty-ounce glasses. Or you can always order a hamburger with fixings at the burger bar. Peggy serves "real" french fries and onion rings. But the most wonderful items are the iced-down, long-neck beers (reminiscent of ice houses) and six-ounce bottled Cokes. You can also choose homemade lemonade. But that's not all. All the desserts are homemade: tarts (65¢), fruit-filled turnovers ($1), gooey chocolate brownies (75¢), and cheesecake.

What more could one ask for? We intend to pack up the whole family and make a regular trip to Wharton from Houston—especially during the town's celebration of Octoberfest.

On the square
(409) 532-5839
Monday—Saturday 11 a.m.—9:30 p.m.

Winedale

WINEDALE CAFE

*T*here are two buildings in Winedale. This is the other one. We labeled it "a tin building that wears many hats." What other cafe have we listed that sells groceries, has video machines, a jukebox, a dance floor (when they push the tables back), and serves a menu that ranges from hamburgers to fresh-prepared seafood and is located 100 yards from a forty-four-acre lake?

We repeatedly asked owner Marilyn Wagner, "Who is going to eat all of this cooking?" She assured us that they have a lot of business from all around. And they have good food, too. *Texas Monthly* magazine's Patricia Sharpe has written, "They serve hamburgers and cheeseburgers that are out of this world." She's right—but that's not all. On Thursday nights you can have either chicken-fried steak or fried catfish filet. They are served with Texas toast, hushpuppies, french fries, and a green salad—all you can eat for $5.95.

Across from the Historical Center
(409) 249-3505
Wednesday–Sunday–9 a.m.–9 p.m.

Woodville

THE MIDDLE BUSTER

*T*he Middle Buster sits on the edge of the Big Thicket Garden. You don't get that effect, though, until you go in. The back of this barbecue cafe is all glass, and it lends a view of birds and animals indigenous to these parts. The Big Thicket Garden is a half-acre tract of land that has most of the ecological environments contained in the Big Thicket National Park. In an hour you can view more than fifty plants, such as granddaddy magnolias, sassafras trees, lilies, gum trees, and many more species from the national park. A natural spring-fed branch marks a lazy course along sloping trails where feeders for birds, small animals, and deer have been placed.

Perhaps working with this as a backdrop is why Carrell Die serves the mouth-watering barbecue he does. We had brisket, dirty rice, and home-cooked pinto beans seasoned with meat, peppers and onions, for $4.50. The brisket melted in our mouths. Carrell cooks his brisket in a pit next to the smokehouse (where sausage and bacon are smoked). When we asked how he learned to cook, Carrell, a propane gas truck driver by profession, said he just asked the Lord, "Lord, I want a little cafe, the Lord said do this and this and this— and that's what I did." Be sure to ask Carrell where the name "The Middle Buster" comes from. It's a story he tells best. (A clue: when you walk up to the door, his Daddy's plough is sitting on the right side.)

Carrell's wife says, "There is no place prettier than Texas, so if you take your barbecue plate out and eat, or walk the garden trail, please don't litter."

US Hwy. 190
(409) 283-5249
Monday—Saturday 11 a.m.—8 p.m.

PICKETT HOUSE

*T*he Pickett House has often served as a pleasant dining spot for tourists who have spent a day visiting the Alabama-Coushatta Indian Reservation, the Big Thicket National Forest, and Heritage Garden—a collection of pioneer buildings that includes a log cabin built in 1866, a working gristmill, a whiskey still, and a blacksmith shop. There are more than two dozen buildings in all, with plenty to see and do.

The Pickett House restaurant is situated in Heritage Village, and it offers the diner one of the best fried chicken family-style dinners in all of East Texas. For around $7 you get chicken and dumplings, fried chicken, three country vegetables—usually butter beans, mustard greens, and sweet potatoes—along with coleslaw, homemade hot biscuits, cornbread, tomato relish, watermelon rind preserves, fruit cobbler, coffee or tea, and fresh buttermilk.

The building itself is partly an old schoolhouse built in 1906. You can easily observe the structure's original floor and the stove that was used for warmth in the winter. There is also an interesting display of circus posters—the collection of Bubba Voss, a trumpet player for twenty-two years in various touring circuses. The restaurant serves its guests family-style on long wooden tables, so be prepared to say "Hi, neighbor." On Friday nights they serve only fried catfish (all you can eat for $7.50).

The restaurant is owned by Don Crain and manager Donna Kucera.

US Hwy. 190 (1 mi. west)
(409) 283-8895
March—August, open seven
days, 11 a.m.—8 p.m.
September—February,
Monday—Thursday 11 a.m.—3 p.m.;
Friday—Sunday 11 a.m.—8 p.m.

South

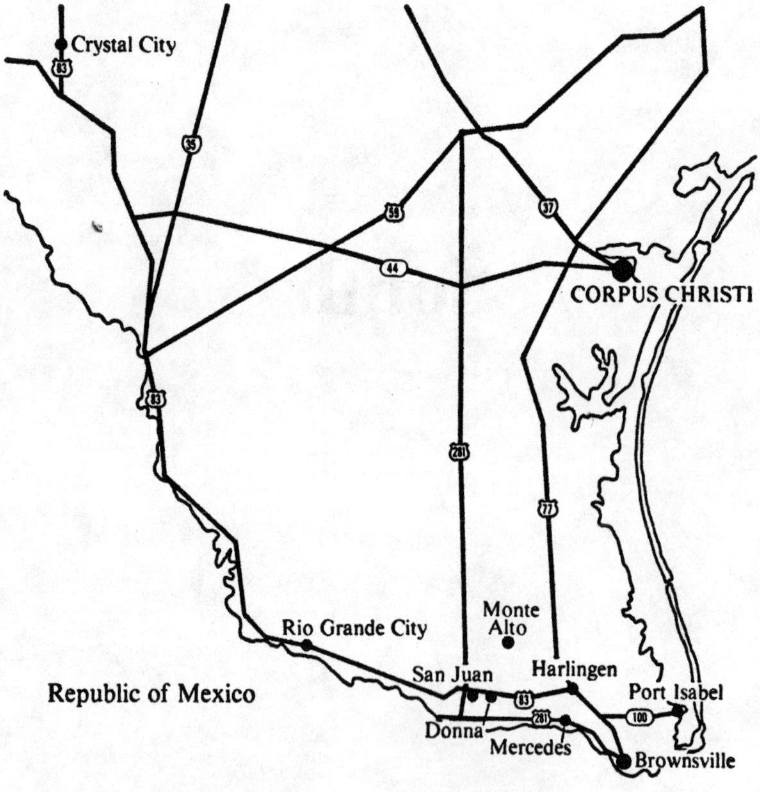
Crystal City
83
35
59
37
44
CORPUS CHRISTI
83
281
77
Monte Alto
Rio Grande City
San Juan
Harlingen
Republic of Mexico
Port Isabel
83
281
100
Donna
Mercedes
Brownsville

Brownsville

CHECKERS CAFE

*J*oe Kenney met his future bride by chance at a convenience store in Houston. Little did Joe imagine that nine years later he and his wife, Nora Liza, would own one of the most successful cafes in Brownsville.

As you can readily tell from the exterior, the Checkers Cafe was once a residence. Today on the inside it is decorated with posters of such movie stars as Humphrey Bogart and Marilyn Monroe. The tables have black and white checked tablecloths, and all the waiters wear Vans, those trendy shoes that, yes, are black and white checked.

But even if the decor borders on being a bit—well, black and white—Checkers still serves some very interesting food. Joe is from Philadelphia, which accounts for why so much of the menu has an East Coast twist. Checkers is home of the Philly Cheese Steak Sandwich. For those of you who don't know, this sandwich begins with boneless chuck that is chopped while it's being cooked. Then cheese is melted on top with grilled onions, and all of it is put into a torpedo-shaped roll. Joe also serves Italian Hoagie sandwiches, as well as a Mexican buffet of cheese enchiladas, rice, beans, and, depending on the day, a meat entrée of either mole, carne guisada, or milaneza.

Of interest to us was the bizzare copper sculpture on the wall, which we finally recognized as the likeness of Elvis Presley, created by none other than the owner. You'll like the 1940s and 1950s music played here.

Corner of 8th and Washington
(512) 542-9721
Monday—Friday 7 a.m.—4 p.m.
Saturday 7 a.m.—3 p.m.

Crystal City

TAVERN RESTAURANT

*I*f you travel through Crystal City, try to arrange your trip so you have a stop late in the afternoon. The Tavern Restaurant does not open until 5 p.m. The restaurant's recipes have been selected for Ann Greer's *Creative Mexican Cooking* and mentioned in *Gourmet Guide to Good Eating*. Owner Ruben Lopez and his wife Carmella oversee each dish served "to make sure the cooks are doing it our way."

The La Tampiqueña is Mrs. Lopez's specialty sauce. Among its uses is to smother shrimp, for Shrimp La Tampiqueña. Served with rice, beans, guacamole, and warm flour tortillas, it costs $8.50. The Lopezes also serve Steak La Tampiqueña, which is strip sirloin and one enchilada, served with rice, beans, and guacamole, for $8.75. They also serve a fifty-three-ounce sirloin that feeds up to three people at a time for $21.85. There are other steaks: T-bones, clubs, and sirloins. Or you can choose a seafood platter or Flounder Veracruz. If you are in the mood for dessert, ask for one of the cobblers, fresh daily.

Ruben exclaims, "We serve the best food in this area!" You'll agree.

FM Rd. 65 (3/10 mi. south)
(512) 374-3116
Tuesday—Sunday 5 p.m.—10:30 p.m.

Donna

HAROLD'S COUNTRY KITCHEN

*I*f you ever needed a party catered in the Valley for, say, a couple of thousand, you would probably wind up calling Harold's Country Kitchen. Fact is, Harold's is about the only operation able to handle that size party. We saw Harold's catering trucks in Brownsville and on the highway to Harlingen. But if a big summer blowout isn't your thing, you can still find out what all the commotion is about by dropping into the establishment itself.

To call this restaurant merely a kitchen is like calling the *Queen Mary* a boat. Harold's is in reality a beautiful white stucco rambling house with spacious green lawns and tall banana trees everywhere. It's peaceful here, almost oasis-like. You can tell that this is an important restaurant from the fact that a room that can handle more than four hundred has been added to the original house.

Harold's is a buffet-style restaurant. For lunch you can choose from six different meat entrées, four different fresh vegetables (don't forget, you're in the Valley, where many of the vegetables we eat are grown in the first place), and four different desserts. Dinner is equally tempting. The specific items vary with the day, but you can generally depend on some sort of ribs, fried chicken, beef tips, liver, and barbecued beef. You'll find some regional favorites as well, such as King Ranch chicken casserole, enchiladas, and chalupas.

To discourage food hogs and wastefulness in the buffet line, a sign plainly reads: "Only take what you can eat." Like all buffet or cafeteria restaurants, the appeal here is vast variety at good value. Lunch costs about $5 and dinner about $1 more.

A testament to this restaurant's popularity among local as well as winter Texans is that the room for four hundred was booked for all of December, January, February, and March. Take note that we visited the restaurant in July. The only thing we found missing was the luxury of being able to sit in large wooden lawn chairs outside underneath a big Texas starry night and be fanned by moving banana tree fronds.

211 E. Old US Hwy. 83
(512) 464-2185
Open seven days, 11 a.m.–8:30 p.m.

Harlingen

VANNIE TILDEN'S BAKERY AND COFFEE SHOP

*H*oused in what was once a Goodyear Service Center, this local institution has long been famous for its baked goods and special-occasion cakes and as a breakfast and lunch spot. Two eggs, grits, baked ham, and fresh, hot biscuits cost about $4. Their waffles are notorious because they are made with real whipped cream.

Vannie Tilden started baking in Atlanta, selling five or six loaves of bread a day. The business grew in Georgia to some twenty-five bakeries but was wiped out in the Great Depression. Not discouraged, Vannie and her husband moved to Brownsville and opened a bakery in 1930. In 1948 the family opened another bakery in Harlingen, just a couple of blocks from its present location.

The bakery is now owned by Fred Deyo (Vannie Tilden's son) and Valerie Deyo. Their product is pretty much summed up by the sign we found on the wall: "We spare no effort to give you the best in home-baked quality. Our products are like a housewife would make them in her kitchen."

Lunch revolves around fresh-made soup, sandwiches, hamburgers, and poorboys. Never forget that Vannie Tilden's is a bakery first, a place in which to eat second.

202 E. Harrison
(512) 423-4062
Monday—Friday 7 a.m.—6 p.m.
Saturday 7 a.m.—5 p.m.

Mercedes

MEXTEX CAFE

*T*his hole-in-the-wall cafe sits along a much-traveled highway between Harlingen and McAllen that has hundred-year-old palm trees swaying in the Gulf breezes. If you don't speak Spanish you won't enjoy the lyrics to the music on the jukebox, but you can still tap your foot along with the beat. Ordering is simple: enchiladas $2.45; three beef tacos $1.85; fried chicken, three pieces $2.50 or five pieces for $4.50. Ten-ounce bottled soft drinks served in glasses with crushed ice cost 60¢. Fresh-brewed iced tea garnished with a lime is 45¢.

Lupita Cantu has operated this tidy cantina for forty years. Her son helps now, and one of his duties is making the fresh-baked pies that are served daily.

Lupita has a vast collection of miniature elephants. It's in the corner in a display cabinet that also houses family pictures and mementos.

Old US Hwy. 83
No phone
Open Wednesday—Monday 9 a.m.—1 p.m.

Monte Alto

MAGUE'S CAFE

*I*f you are just driving through but still want to satisfy your palate, Mague's is for you. With hamburgers, Mexican food, fried fish, and onion rings or french fries as your choices, you won't be hungry long. You'll be picnicking with other happy diners consisting of fellow tourists, fishermen, boaters, and just plain hungry local folk.

FM Rd. 88
(512) 262-3270
Open seven days, 11 a.m.—7 p.m.

Port Isabel

FISHERMAN'S INN

*T*he unassuming exterior of this cafe might tempt you to pass it up. Trust us. You'd miss a great meal and lots of fun.

In these parts Peggy Reeves is known as the singing waitress. In her backless knit dress and stiletto heels, she serves and sings all at once. While we were heading for our table, a young man played "Harper Valley PTA" on the jukebox. You can imagine the look on our faces when Peggy began unabashedly belting out the words along with Jeannie C. Riley—handing us menus, silverware, and water and never missing a beat.

You sit at tables whose tops have been decorated with color and black and white snapshots of various local fishing feats. The menu item eaten here most frequently is the perfect bite-size fried shrimp (approximately three dozen in a serving), coleslaw, and iced tea, all for $5.95. Still hungry? You can have another order for an additional $1.

This is a family place with a capital F. We saw lots of kids wearing T-shirts that proclaimed, "Life is a Beach." We agree that it should be.

Texas Hwy. 100
(512) 943-9983
Open seven days, 5 a.m.–10 p.m.

ISABEL'S CAFE

*T*he sign outside this cafe does not depict a misguided flying saucer (though we had to ask). Rather, it is supposed to be a flour tortilla with eggs and potato, just one of Isabel Gonzales's choice breakfast items. The Contodo is the best-selling breakfast taco for $3 and an original idea of Isabel's. You get a fresh homemade flour tortilla with a filling of refried beans, ground beef, lettuce, tomato, onion, and chili con carne. Or you can order their flour tortilla with potato and egg for $1.75 or chorizo and eggs for $2.

If your breakfast mood has been squelched from a preoccupation with early morning shell hunting, you can have one of Isabel's good Mexican food plate lunches: three enchiladas for $2.75, three tacos for $1.75, or maybe an order of flour tortillas with a pat of butter for 75¢.

You can't miss Isabel's sign, but if you should, just ask the locals where the cafe is. Isabel's twelve years in business have made her a well-known local figure.

Texas Hwy. 100 at Port Isabel Rd.
(512) 943-5082
Monday—Saturday 6 a.m.—4 p.m.
Sunday 7 a.m.—2 p.m.

Rio Grande City

CARO'S

*M*aybe some of the charm of this restaurant is just the adventure of finding it. Even though Rio Grande City isn't large, Caro's isn't all that easy to locate. But here's how. Just go west on Second Street until you spot a small cemetery and a Firestone sign on your left; on your right will be a large sign for Caro's. Turn right, and a short distance away you'll find it.

What a pretty little spot Caro's is. It reminded us a lot of real Mexico. The street on which it is situated is very narrow, with barely enough room for two cars. You will be struck by the beauty of the scene outside: pink bougainvillea, an olive tree, cacti, and a small adobe house. The colors are green, brown, yellow, red, and pink—a symphony of Mexican hues.

Juan and Carmine Caro go to great lengths to bring you some of the best Tex-Mex food in this part of Texas—maybe the best. Understand that these people don't even own a can opener. That means that everything they prepare is as fresh as possible. Corn for the tortillas is ground fresh daily. They even grind their own spices used in the kitchen—whole comino, oregano, pepper, and garlic—in a *molcajete*. The specialty of the house is a puffy tostada that was developed by Juan's mother, who founded the restaurant in 1938 in order to support her six children. A portrait of

Juan's mother is on display behind the cash register, as if even today she is casting a careful eye on the quality of the food and a keen one on the money.

Dining tips: another specialty is the Spanish rice. It is soaked in chicken broth and flavored with many different Mexican spices. The green sauce on the table is best eaten between bites of food. It is hot and not for the timid.

Disregard the long rattlesnake over the entrance to the restrooms. He's quite dead.

Prices at Caro's are very reasonable. The Caro's Special, which includes practically everything you could possibly want, is only $4.50.

Caro's has been visited by Senator Edward Kennedy and Governor Allan Shivers. It's definitely worth your presence, too.

205 N. Garcia
(512) 487-2255
Monday—Saturday
11 a.m.—2 p.m. and 5—9 p.m.
Sunday 11 a.m.—2 p.m.
and 3 p.m.—9 p.m.

San Juan

GARZA CAFE

*T*his is a most forbidding building. Nobody in his or her right mind would enter this place except if someone of good authority told them it was okay. We're telling you it's okay. Never mind the bars on the window and the shabby exterior; just walk right in. The owners are friendly and the food exceptionally good. In fact, the cafe has been in operation for more than forty years by Josefa Garza. She was widowed at thirty and started the restaurant to support her seven children. Today the cafe is managed by Josefa's daughter, Alicia Salinas.

Garza's has grown from a stand-up lunch counter to a cafe providing true sit-down dining.

Like many cafes down here in the Rio Grande Valley, this one specializes in Tex-Mex food. The Garza Cafe's tortillas are homemade, along with the enchilada sauce, which is prepared from red chilis right in the kitchen. On Saturday the Garza serves *cabrito* (goat), rice, beans, salad, and tortillas for just $4.95. For the most part, you dine with locals in the know and a few winter Texans if it's the season. Have no fear. It's worth the experience.

308 N. Nebraska
(512) 787-9051
Tuesday—Friday
11 a.m.—3 p.m. and 4:30 p.m.—8 p.m.
Saturday 10 a.m.—9 p.m.
Sunday 8 a.m.—8 p.m.

West

152

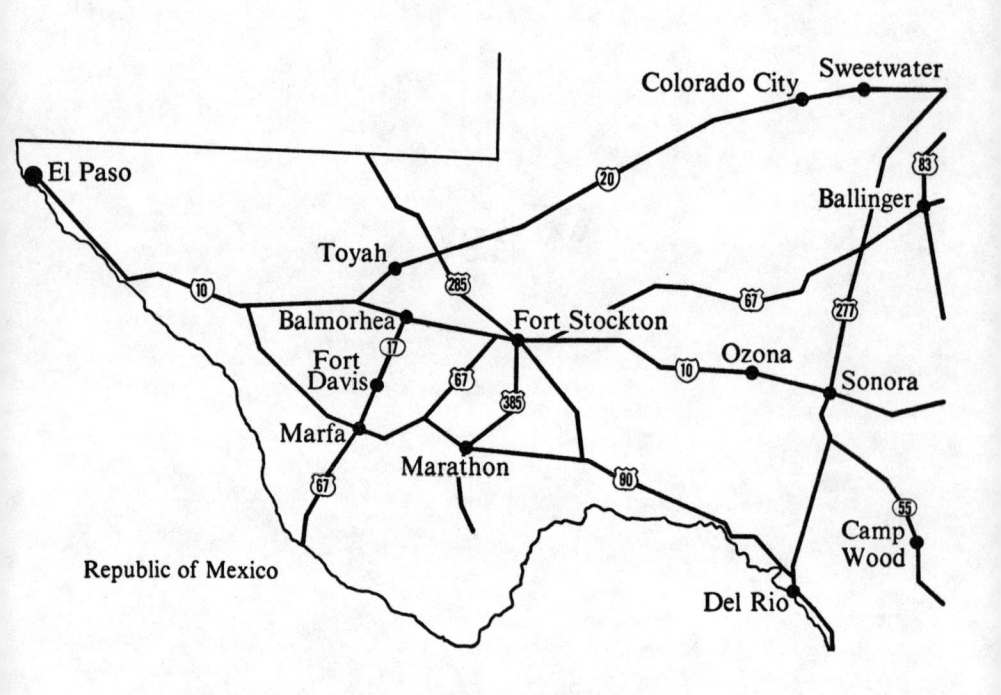

Ballinger

FRIENDLY CORNER CAFE

We still had a lump in our throats when we ambled into the Friendly Corner. Driving through town we had stopped at the picturesque square to see the bronze statue by Pompeo Coppini. In their only son's memory, the Noyes, who were early settlers in these parts, had the statue erected to attest to the hardships of a young cowboy's life. We were told that Charles Noyes was killed when the horse on which he was riding reared and threw him.

But the lingering traces of melancholy quickly left us as we settled ourselves into one of the many turquoise booths at the Friendly. This was clearly a cafe that lives up to its name. Jennifer, a recent graduate of Ballinger High School, was one of the sweetest waitresses we had had. As we were munching on grilled 100 percent beef hamburgers, Jennifer proceeded to tell us what the Friendly was all about. We quickly learned that the cafe was the center for many of Ballinger's activities. Every Wednesday morning the Ballinger Bearcat football team "always have" eaten breakfast in the back dining room. They used to have lunch there, too, but now the cheerleaders provide lunch in the school's gym. The back room is also where the Sunday school teachers' monthly meeting is held. The Friendly is a gathering spot for locals, and we found it to provide great rancher-watching. The long table on the left side was obviously the regulars' haven. Owner Ruth Walker called it the "bull table" or "hot-air table." Everybody "makes themselves at home, and they talk over cattle, football, baseball, or whatever."

Good food is a priority here, too. Our hamburger was served on a grilled bun garnished with crispy lettuce, a better-than-average tomato, pickle, and onion for $1.75. The beef is from the local meat company—a guarantee of freshness. The home-style french fries were a generous portion for 50¢, as was the fresh-brewed tea for 35¢. We had a hearty lunch.

Of course, there are lunch specials, too. That day diners had a choice of chicken-fried steak or turkey and dressing, two vegetables, a salad, cornbread, and tea or coffee for $3.25. Mattie's famous desserts are included, too—rice pudding, an assortment of cake choices, or maybe chocolate pudding. Mattie has been here for years and takes all this cooking in stride. A regular chortled, "Tell them one thing. Don't bang your cup on the table when you want another cup of coffee. Ruth doesn't like that." Ruth has it under control.

Texas Hwy. 158
(915) 365-2424
Monday–Friday 6 a.m.–6 p.m.
Saturday and Sunday 7 a.m.–1:30 p.m.

Balmorhea

CHICKEN CHARLIE'S

*B*almorhea is a small town. So you have to understand that Chicken Charlie's could easily be described as a major miracle. Obviously nobody ran any complicated marketing studies on this one, for if they had, the restaurant would never have existed. But despite its isolation, Chicken Charlie's is a great experience. Every inch of the interior is covered with ranch memorabilia, from branding irons to barbed wire to gimme caps to you name it. We were told that many of the improvements to the building and the vast collection of ranch stuff is the work of the owner, Art Climer.

What's really put Art on the map, though, is his chicken-fried steak served with thick cream gravy, mountains of french fries, and salad. On Sunday they serve fried chicken. Don't overlook the homemade pies cooked by Mrs. Cecil Kingston, a longtime Balmorhea rancher's wife. She bakes apple, cherry, coconut, chocolate, pecan, and, especially on Sundays, strawberry pies.

Of interest to us were the menus, which are merely school tablets in which someone has hand-printed the items--named, by the way, for some of Art's best customers. For example, we have the Joe Gallegos: "A good friend, good Pearl drinker, pretty good J.P., fair bean cooker and a hell of a nice guy." The Joe Gallegos is chicken strips served with fried or baked potato, salad, cream gravy, and Texas toast.

This is the kind of place that would make a small fortune appealing to the drugstore cowboy set in a place like Dallas. The difference is, this is the real thing.

Don't miss Connie Climer's gift shop on the second floor. And by the way, Art's got a car wash, an RV park, and a laundromat in the complex as well.

Although we didn't try it, we suspect that the bob white quail dinner, even at a pricey $18.95, is excellent. Most dinners are in the $6−7 range.

If you're ever headed this way, don't pass Chicken Charlie's by.

Main St., off IH 10
(915) 375-2433
Open seven days, noon−8 p.m.

Camp Wood

OLD TIMER

Once you've been to Camp Wood, you can easily see why even somebody from as pretty a spot as Corpus Christi might want to move here. This is Edwards Plateau country. The land comprises wooded hills, steep rocky cliffs, secluded valleys, and clear running streams. The views are postcard-like, and the air is something that could be bottled and sold to New Yorkers.

Eight years ago the Milliorns, Pat and Bea, retired here to own and operate the Old Timer restaurant. Pat had been a career Navy man stationed in Corpus Christi.

Although the menu is varied, the specialty of the house is chicken-fried steak, a fact confirmed almost daily by residents of Uvalde who drive the thirty-eight miles just to eat here. The six-ounce chicken-fried is hand-breaded and comes with homemade french fries or a Texas-size baked potato, lettuce and tomato salad, and homemade cream gravy. For $4.35, it's not just a good value, it's also a great meal. Desserts include homemade pies as well as Bea's famous Cinderella cake—made with pumpkin and frosted with buttercream icing. It's a treasured family recipe, so Bea would not share the details.

The Old Timer is open for breakfast, lunch, and dinner, and on Sunday there's a buffet. Famous people who have eaten here include Don Williams and Joe Namath.

Before you leave Camp Wood, be sure and visit the park. In it you'll find a plaque describing how Charles Lindberg, while lost flying west in 1923, landed on a Camp Wood street and, upon taking off again, crashed his airplane into a local building. Maybe he flew over the spot where the Old Timer is now.

Texas Hwy. 55
(512) 597-2112
Tuesday—Sunday 6 a.m.—10 p.m.

Colorado City

TAYLOR'S TRUCK TOWN

*Y*ou can eat here; the menu is respectable, with such dishes as fried catfish, Mexican food, fried chicken, steaks, and barbecue. But the foremost reason to stop is to check out the mural that artist Eustace painted in 1967. Sip a Coke and muse over the West Texas desert scene. It's the most art we've seen on an inside wall in any cafe we visited.

IH 20 at Texas Hwy. 208
(915) 728-5325
Open seven days, 24 hours

Del Rio

MEMO'S

*T*he most important thing we can tell you about Memo's is that it's owned by Blondie Calderon. Country and western music afficionados might know that Blondie plays piano, vibes, and drums for Ray Price. The walls of this restaurant are decorated with pictures of Blondie's musical friends, including Kris Kristofferson, Johnny Rodriguez, and many others.

Like so many restaurants in this part of Texas, Memo's specializes in Mexican food. You can find basic enchiladas, tacos, or chalupas or, if you're more adventurous, Portuguese tortillas and *pericos*—a sort of loaded nacho. The restaurant offers hamburgers, steaks, and sandwiches as well.

Situated on the banks of the San Felipe Creek, this border-town restaurant is an institution, having been operated by Blondie's family for more than forty years.

804 Losoya
(512) 775-8104
Monday–Saturday 11 a.m.–2 p.m.
and 5 p.m.–10 p.m.
Sundays 5 p.m.–10 p.m.

MEXICAN KITCHEN

*A*cross the street from Memo's is the Mexican Kitchen. While perhaps not as famous, we think their food has equal footing. Every noon there is a buffet line that lets you ponder fajitas, *encebolladas* (beef sirloin strips grilled with onions), beef or cheese enchiladas, beef or chicken flautas, red and green (miniversion) *chimichangas*, beef taco fixings, chili con carne, mashed beans, Spanish rice, guacamole, jalapeños, and homemade flour tortillas to wrap it all up in if you like. This vast array of Tex-Mex costs $4.95 at lunch and $5.95 at dinner.

A retired schoolteacher, Berta Medina has been operating this cafe since 1970 with the help of her mother and the rest of the Medina clan. "Running a cafe is a lot more challenging than teaching. I've met so many nice people, and we've never had a dissatisfied customer."

The reason, we suspect, is that she serves a good product in a friendly atmosphere. That spells success.

807 E. Losoya
(512) 774-2280
Open seven days, 11 a.m.–2 p.m.
and 5 p.m.–10 p.m.

El Paso

FARMER'S MARKET CAFE

*T*he old wooden bench in front of the Farmer's Market Cafe is a fine place to ponder the changes that twenty-odd years have brought. At one time the site was on the edge of El Paso, surrounded by farms—thus the name. Today the big white stucco building sits at a major intersection, surrounded by commercial enterprises. But it still has the feel of a small-town cafe. The proprietor, Tino Hernandez, leases the space by the month. The building's owner hopes to sell the land to a supermarket or chain store and cash in big, so the cafe could disappear any day.

Although the popular attraction here is barbecued brisket (which can be a tad dry), the *huevos rancheros* breakfast is a bargain. It consists of one or two fried eggs on a tortilla liberally doused with freshly made Spanish sauce and grated white cheese, hash browns (these are real fried potato patties), and homemade refried beans, flanked by extra flour tortillas and a mug of hot coffee, all for $2.55. The day we ate there we were served by a pleasant waiter with a mere eighteen-year tenure. On any particular day the special might be spareribs, hot links, Swiss steak, tacos, or chicken-fried steak, with three vegetables, for $2.75. The soup every Friday is, always has been, and always will be, fish chowder. The

Farmer's Market has even had a sports star, golfer Lee Trevino, as a customer.

5013 Doniphan
(915) 584-3415
Tuesday—Sunday 7 a.m.—8 p.m.
Monday 7 a.m.—3 p.m.

Fort Davis

BOARDING HOUSE RESTAURANT

*T*he first thing we discovered about West Texas is the transformation that takes place within us because we are there. We're not sure exactly how or why this phenomenon happens, but it does. In West Texas, everybody is friendly. People wave to you from passing cars. Maybe people are friendly here because West Texas is such a big open space.

Fort Davis, population less than eight hundred, is definitely West Texas. This is big country where ranches are measured in sections rather than acres (a section is 640 acres). It is with a degree of gratefulness, then, that we came upon the Boarding House Restaurant. Sutler's Limpia Hotel is behind it.

Lunch or dinner at the Boarding House is a choice of steaks, pork chops, or, of course, a pretty good chicken-fried steak. There are homemade pies and chocolate sundaes for dessert, too. But for our money, breakfast here is what you should aim for. Less than $5 can get you a breakfast buffet that includes bacon, sausage, scrambled eggs, toast, biscuits, flapjacks, juice, and coffee or hot tea. This is the same type of chow that ranch hands eat.

We were particularly interested in the Sutler Smoothies—a blender specialty made with yogurt, apple juice, a banana, and frozen strawberries or blackberries. Yes, this is a lot like something you'd expect to find in Los Angeles, and not normally in cowboy country. But you'll agree that it's refreshing and nutritious—a perfect start to a day that might include hiking in Big Bend National Park. Maybe it's the fresh air or the serenity or both, but we found ourselves eating more and feeling guiltless about it during our stay.

Don't miss historic Fort Davis, a few miles away, or the Indian Lodge, built after the Great Depression as a means of getting people back to work. The lodge is in the style of pueblo architecture and is located within the Davis Mountains State Park.

The Boarding House Restaurant is owned by Mac and Judy Sproul.

Texas Hwy. 17
(915) 426-3241
Open seven days, 11 a.m.–3 p.m.
and 6 p.m.–9:30 p.m.

Fort Stockton

RAILSBACK CAFE

*F*riendliness is what the Railsback Cafe owners are all about. Lem and Doris Railsback have been serving up a lot of friendliness to their customers for more than sixteen years. Lem purchased this quaint cafe built from Austin rock after working for forty-seven years for other eating establishments. Even though the interstate passed them by a couple of years back, travelers who know still take time to stop on their way to other destinations. It's is a great way to drop in on the local atmosphere of Fort Stockton. While you dine you can plug into the local gossip by listening to ranchers, oil and gas people, and farmers discussing which gas well is producing how much gas or how it would be good if the weather would break.

Lem's previous restaurant experience has provided him with the ability to do it all, he says. But, "I don't like to fool with Mexican food too much. I know I have stiff competition." He just cooks food that keeps people coming back. His chicken-fried steak has no competition: breaded in flour, dipped in egg and milk, and then breaded again, each morsel is mouth-watering good and is covered in Lem's own cream gravy. You can't go wrong. It's served with homemade mashed potatoes, a dried bean dish (pinto or white), a vegetable, homemade soup, salad, hot homemade rolls, and cornbread, all for $4.65. That is a good value. (Lem shared his recipes with me. He says, "If someone tells you it's a secret recipe, it is because they're guessing at it.")

If you are getting an early start, try the breakfast order of a stack of three pancakes for $3.95, with a side order of ham, sausage, or bacon. Pancakes are another of Lem's specialties. There is also cinnamon toast, French toast, biscuits, and dry or cooked cereal. All this food can be consumed while you're taking in his son's color photographs of West Texas that hang on the walls. You can even purchase them.

Lem's wife Doris is the friendliest cashier in Texas. She'll talk nonstop to you about the weather, her nine grandchildren, her five great-grandchildren, or her real love (besides Lem), fishing—all this while pleasantly taking your money. Lem tattles, "Doris would rather fish than eat," and it would seem that she would rather dance, too. The way Lem tells it, "Why, Doris did the jitterbug for me just last night."

Lem must be living right. He says, "At seventy-one, there is no other way to live." Amen!

710 W. Dickinson
(915) 336-2863
Monday–Saturday 6 a.m.–9 p.m.

SARAH'S CAFE

*C*leo Castelo, who with her husband Mike owns Sarah's Cafe, is Fort Stockton's self-appointed ambassador of goodwill. She sees to it that first-time lady visitors receive a complimentary miniature Mexican pot and a *quesadilla*. (Men get only the *quesadilla*). While tallying up your check, she will tell you to call her collect if you have car trouble on the highway, and her guest register has signatures from all over the world.

It never ceases to amaze us how Mexican restaurants can take five ingredients and turn them into forty-five different meals. Sarah's is no exception. Here your lunch starts with tostadas made at the cafe. The green and red chile sauces are prepared from a recipe handed down by Cleo's mother, who started the restaurant in 1929. Cleo guards the recipe so closely that she goes in early to prepare it when nobody else is around.

Unfortunately, the red chile sauce was a touch too tomatoey for us, and the enchiladas with green sauce were soggy. The fresh guacamole was exceptionally good, however.

106 S. Nelson
(915) 336-7124
Monday—Saturday 11 a.m.—2 p.m.
and 5 p.m.—9 p.m.
Closed major holidays

Marathon

GAGE HOTEL RESTAURANT

*T*he Gage Hotel was built in 1927 by Alfred Gage, himself a Texas rancher and businessman, as a stopping place for other travelers. In 1982 the hotel, by then in a declining state, was purchased and restored by Houstonians J. P. and Mary Jon Bryan.

The hotel, including its annex, has nineteen rooms furnished with antiques and named after Big Bend National Park landmarks or famous people who were instrumental in settling Texas. In the Stillwell's Crossing Room you will find a two-hundred-year-old brass bed and in the Persimmon Gap Room an antique four-poster bed.

Downstairs in the dining room, don't be surprised to encounter hungry Texans who have driven from Alpine, Fort Stockton, or Singleton. In this part of Texas people don't seem bothered about driving a couple of hours to eat.

The menu changes on the daily chalkboard, but manager Giddings Brown has fresh fish flown in from the Gulf, generally including red snapper, trout, and shrimp for tempura. It's picked up in Fort Stockton, fifty-eight miles away, driven to Marathon, and prepared for you. A chicken-fried steak with baked potato or french fries, green salad, vegetables, and rolls costs $7.95. Homemade desserts include pecan pie at

$1.50 a slice. Other items from the kitchen are steaks, hamburgers, sandwiches, fried chicken, and Mexican food.

Half the fun of eating here is enjoying the history of the hotel and the peaceful surroundings of a small town miles from anywhere else. A romantic notion to think over: Zane Grey spent a month writing in this hotel.

US Hwy. 90
(915) 386-4205
Open seven days, 7 a.m.—2 p.m.
and 5:30 p.m.—9 p.m.

Marfa

OLD BORUNDA CAFE

*B*y now Carolina Borunda Humphries' cafe may be the best-known obscure cafe in Texas. The fare is basic enchiladas and tamales in a ubiquitous chili gravy of astonishing orange hue. Everybody in the county eats at this tidy white diner, from young families with crying tots to cowboys with spurs that jingle-jangle-jingle. We have only one word to say to you: pralines—luscious, brittle morsels of brown sugar and pecans made by Carolina's niece. These world-class candies will soothe you mightily on the rest of your journey across West Texas. Don't neglect to lay in an adequate supply. There's nothing worse than reaching over to grab another and finding that you ate the last one along about San Angelo.

203 San Antonio
(915) 729-4338
Hours vary

Ozona

PEPE'S RESTAURANT

*P*epe's Restaurant is not an art gallery, yet you'll find some of the best pen and ink drawings in all of West Texas here. The drawings are the work of Alfredo Torbar, owner of Pepe's; some sell for more than $500 apiece. The day we were there, we saw a likeness of Judge Roy Bean, several good courthouses, and a drawing of an old West Texas windmill.

Alfredo and his wife Lisa cook the food themselves, because, as he puts it, "No one else will do it right."

The specialty of the house is the *huevos rancheros* breakfast with homemade flour tortillas, beans, homemade hash browns, and bacon or sausage, along with scrambled eggs covered with homemade chunky hot sauce, for $3.

Lunch and dinner provide a chance to sample some of Lisa and Alfredo's other Mexican specialties, such as enchiladas, tacos, and their refried beans. Alfredo points with delight at his hot sauce, which is made from an old family recipe. It's "Texas hot," he says. We agree.

Pepe's menu also carries more traditional items such as burgers, sandwiches, pork chops, and steaks, but for our money we would stick to what Alfredo and Lisa seem to like best—Tex-Mex.

Across from the restaurant, be sure to pay homage to the monument of Texas liberty fighter Davy Crockett, for whom the county is named. Ozona is the county seat.

US Hwy. 290
(915) 392-2906
Monday—Saturday 7 a.m—10 p.m.

Sonora

COMMERCIAL RESTAURANT

*F*or three generations the Lopezes have owned and operated the Commercial Restaurant. That's a total of fifty years, and Gloria and Lemuel Lopez have operated the restaurant for the last twelve. That's a lot of days making some of the best Tex-Mex food in these parts.

One of the most popular items served, and one we consider a real taste treat, is their homemade tamales served awash in chili gravy (six tamales for $2.50). Or try a side dish of guacamole (real chunks of avacado abound) for $2. Or maybe the eighteen-year veteran waitress Tina will guide you to the all-encompassing Deluxe Mexican Dinner. It's a lot of good food: guacamole, chili con queso, soft beef tacos, bean chalupas, refried beans, Spanish rice, cheese enchiladas, and beef enchiladas (all made on the premises) for $5.20.

This is a neat and clean operation. Lemuel says, "Cleanliness seems to be our motto." Before you leave, trying to decide if you should drive on or take a nap after the food binge, observe the mosaic of fighting roosters. It has been hanging in that very spot for more than twenty years.

154 S. Plum
(915) 387-9928
Tuesday—Saturday 11 a.m.—2:30 p.m.
and 5 p.m.—9 p.m.

Sweetwater

ALLEN'S FAMILY STYLE MEALS

*I*f fried chicken, mashed potatoes, salad, rolls, and homemade peach cobbler is the meal that evokes fond memories of your mother and grandmother, Allen's Family Style Meals is your best bet for happy dining. Allen's has been serving the locals, residents of nearby towns, and hungry well-informed travelers since 1940 in this large one-room eatery. The long tables are placed together in two's and three's, edge to edge, in rows; everyone eats together family-style.

You can help yourself to the brimming bowls of fried chicken and one other meat, and eight vegetables such as corn on the cob, sweetened mashed squash, red beans, green beans, sweet potatoes, okra, and other seasonal vegetable varieties. Your dessert choice is simple, since there is only one: their famous peach cobbler.

1301 E. Broadway
(915) 235-2060
Tuesday–Sunday 11 a.m.–2 p.m.

Toyah

TOYAH TRUCK STOP CAFE

*I*f there were a Burma Shave sign on IH 20 between Pecos and Van Horn, it would read, "Toyah Truck Stop Cafe . . . This is your last chance . . . For 121 miles for home cooked meals . . . Really," and the last one would have a painted vulture on it, to emphasize the point.

Mark and Carolyn Chaddick have been serving truckers, locals, interstate travelers, and every hungry person who has sauntered along for more than thirteen years, with "a lot of return business," Carolyn adds proudly.

Their specialty is pit-cooked barbecue and around-the-clock breakfast service. They serve a sliced beef brisket with homemade potato salad, coleslaw, and Mark's pinto beans on a large "Texas Size Plate" for $5.45. "We've never seen anyone finish it yet," Carolyn claims. Diners' favorite breakfast is a skillet-cooked omelette—either ham and cheese or Spanish. The Spanish omelette is made with Mark's homemade chili and cheese. If you like yours spicy, be sure to ask for the jalapeño-based "super" hot sauce. Omelettes are served with homemade biscuits, grits, or homemade hash browns and cost $3.85. Coffee is 40¢ for all you can drink, or iced tea in a quart glass is 60¢, also for all you can drink.

Cities

Big city dwellers, take heart! When you find yourself hungry for Mom's home cooking but unable to travel country roads to appease your desires, check out this guide to city cafes. Menus range from early breakfasts, thick chicken-fried steaks, and *carne al pastor* to mouth-watering barbecue dishes. You'll leave saying, "Now, that's what I call great food!"

Austin

GOOD EATS CAFE

*G*ood Eats is easy eating. You can go with your editor or the kids and their friends. Almost anything goes—if your palate desires it, they serve it. Casual good food and reasonably priced are the bywords here.

1530 Barton Springs
(512) 476-8141
Sunday–Thursday
11:00 a.m.–11 p.m.
Friday and Saturday
11:00 a.m.–11 p.m.

JAKE'S

*E*stablished in 1948, Jake's has a long history of serving homestyle food. The menu ranges from chicken-fried steak, fried oysters, and nachos to daily specials. Every afternoon, those in the know play shuffleboard.

801 W. 5th
(512) 472-7443
Monday–Friday
7 a.m.–midnight

THREADGILL'S

*L*ocated in a building that dates back to 1933, this institution has been a gas station and a yodelers' and pickers' hangout (Janis Joplin sang here). And now it's a cafe that serves American food, southern style, locally famous for their hand-breaded chicken-fried steak and fresh vegetables. Try their breads and pastries, too, all made from scratch. Bring your quarters and play the great jukebox.

6416 N. Lamar
(512) 451-5440
Monday–Friday
6:30 a.m.–10 p.m.
Saturday and Sunday
6:30 a.m.–10 p.m.

VIRGINIA'S CAFE

*V*irginia cooks and serves a hearty lunch in a no-nonsense way. She is not aiming to win popularity contests. For simple, straightforward dining, Virginia's fills the tab.

S. 1st at El Paso
No phone
Monday–Saturday
11 a.m.–3 p.m.

Corpus Christi

ELMO'S ROADHOUSE INN

*T*his relatively new cafe (established in 1981) serves Corpus Christi its favorite chicken-fried steaks at lunch. At night you can get seafood or steak, followed by homemade desserts. A friendly atmosphere and food with reasonable prices make this a good spot to note.

IH 37 at Violet Rd.
(512) 241-0621
Lunch Tuesday–Sunday
Dinner Tuesday–Saturday

TAQUERIA JALISCO NO. 2

*B*rush up on your Spanish before you eat here. Freshly made Tex-Mex dishes are the fare.

2341 Horne
(512) 855-1162
Monday–Thursday
6 a.m.–11 p.m.
Friday and Saturday
6 a.m.–4 a.m.
Sunday 6 a.m.–midnight

Dallas

BLUE FRONT RESTAURANT

*O*pened in 1877, this is the oldest restaurant in the Southwest. An even more amazing fact is that it has been family-owned and -operated the entire time. Day after day, the menu has remained the same: pig knuckles, corn beef, smoked tongue, greens, coleslaw, boiled potatoes, and hash. There's a lot more, all good, all homestyle and served with a smile.

1310 Elm
(214) 741-7560
Monday–Friday
7:30 a.m.–3:30 p.m.

FARMER'S MARKET RESTAURANT

*A*fter stocking up on fresh vegetables from the Farmer's Market, let the Farmer's Market restaurant show you how to prepare them. Texas farmers have been eating here for more than twenty years.

2011 Taylor
(214) 747-1070
Open seven days,
4 a.m.–9 p.m.

FRAN'S CAFE

*T*here is no escaping the crowds at Fran's. This popular cafe is busy, lunch and dinner. Chicken-fried steak, meat loaf, smothered steak, roast beef, and homemade desserts are merely a few of the mouth-watering choices.

9247 Skillman
(214) 553-1330
Monday–Thursday
11 a.m.–10 p.m.
Friday and Saturday
11 a.m.–11 p.m.
Sunday 11:30 a.m.–10 p.m.

GENNIE'S BISHOP GRILL

*G*ennie's is closed on Saturdays; you should plan all your trips to Dallas during the week. Chicken-fried steaks, catfish filets, roast beef, meat loaf, chili, and beef stew are all served cafeteria style. Businessmen, hardhats, and city officials pack this place daily.

308 N. Bishop
(214) 946-1752
Monday–Friday
11 a.m.–2 p.m.

HIGHLAND PARK CAFETERIA

*T*he Highland Park is not a cafe by Webster's standards. Nonetheless, this cafeteria serves some of the best homestyle meals in Texas. Pound cake, chocolate cream pie, pecan pie, and peach cobbler are a small sample of their to-die-for desserts.

4611 Cole
(214) 526-3801
Monday–Saturday
11 a.m.–8 p.m.

Fort Worth

MASSEY'S

We were told by many people to eat their chicken-fried steak. We tried. Massey's serves a chicken-fried steak that literally covers the plate. With barely room to coexist, there's also mashed potatoes with cream gravy and a vegetable, too

1805 8th Ave.
(817) 924-8242
Open seven days,
7 a.m.—9:45 p.m.

PARIS COFFEE SHOP

*H*ere's a breakfast and lunch spot that serves American-style home-cooked food that's really good. Homemade cookies are one of their specialties—chocolate chip–pecan, oatmeal-raisin-pecan cookies, and German chocolate, to name a few. If it's Thursday, try the chicken and dumplings.

704 W. Magnolia
(817) 335-2041
Monday–Friday
6 a.m.–3 p.m.
Saturday 6 a.m.–11 a.m.

Houston

ANDY'S HOME CAFE

A family-owned and -operated cafe serving home-cooked Tex-Mex food from Andy's mother's well-guarded recipes. During lunch, dine next to businessmen. At night, this is a popular spot for the Rockefeller's and Fitzgerald's crowd. Many times local popular band members have been sighted here.

**1115 E. 11th
(713) 861-9423
Open seven days, 24 hours**

AVALON DRUGSTORE

*R*OHO's (River Oaks Home Owners), car salesmen, businessmen, would-be's, and consummate Yuppies make this their favorite haunt. Thick malts, greasy burgers, homemade fries, a magazine stand with the *New York Times*, freshly squeezed limeade and lemonade, charge accounts, and waitresses like Mary keep bringing them back.

2518 Kirby
(713) 529-9136
Monday–Friday
6:30 a.m.–7 p.m.
Saturday 7 a.m.–5 p.m.
Sunday 8 a.m.–2 p.m.

ELEVENTH STREET CAFE

*N*o flash here, just the opportunity to sample good food in a homey atmosphere.

748 11th
(713) 862-0089
Tuesday–Friday
7 a.m.–3 p.m. and 5–10 p.m.
Saturday and Sunday
8 a.m.–3 p.m. and 5–11 p.m.

LONE STAR CAFE

*T*he Lone Star Cafe has become a popular morning gathering spot for Houston business types. Good food, pleasant service and reasonable prices are the norm.

5591 Richmond
11853 Wilcrest
6211 FM Rd. 1960 W.
Open seven days, breakfast,
lunch, and dinner

MAMA'S CAFE

*M*ama's boasts a bustling, bright atmosphere with customers from all walks of life. On Wednesdays you can eat Texas style: thick chicken-fried steaks and for dessert, Mama's chocolate-chocolate cake.

6019 Westheimer
(713) 266-8514
Monday—Thursday
6:30 a.m.—midnight
Friday 6:30 a.m.—1 a.m.
Saturday 8 a.m.—1 a.m.

SULLY'S

*S*ully's touts the best hamburgers on Highway 6. Their cheesey-burger is the favorite. Fresh homestyle fries, too.

448 Texas Hwy. 6 S.
(713) 497-2023
Monday–Friday
6 a.m.–6:30 p.m.
Saturday 8:30 a.m.–4:30 p.m.

OUISIE'S

*P*ronounced Weesie's, this is a popular inside-the-Loop institution. The menu varies from Oysters Kennard to scallops in Chablis, topped off by thick and gooey desserts. Who can resist? If you don't go early, be prepared to wine leisurely while the repeat customers savor their meals. No reservations.

1708 Sunset
(713) 528-2264
Tuesday–Saturday
11 a.m.–11:30 p.m.

San Antonio

MI TIERRA CAFE AND BAKERY

*O*f all the choices statewide, this is probably our favorite. The breakfast menu is unbeatable, especially the fresh-squeezed orange juice. On the way out there are ample choices of fresh Mexican baked items to choose from.

218 Produce Row
(Market Square)
(512) 225-1262
Open seven days, 24 hours

EARL ABEL'S

*N*ot all places in San Antonio serve only Mexican food. When you have reached your quota, try Earl Abel's, noted for chicken-fried steaks, thick steaks, and homemade french fries.

**4210 Broadway
(512) 822-3358
Open seven days, 24 hours**

DE WESE'S TIP TOP CAFE

*I*n 1938 John and Alvah De Wese opened this simple eatery. The De Wese family still follows their predecessors' standards of cooking. Their chicken-fried steak is among the most popular in Texas; one customer actually packs it into her suitcase on the way to business trips in New York. Their hand-breaded onion rings melt in your mouth, and a slice of their rhubarb pie is a must.

**2814 Fredericksburg
(512) 732-0191
Sunday and
Tuesday–Thursday
11 a.m.–8 p.m.
Friday and Saturday
11 a.m.–9 p.m.**